Strategic Planning and Management
for Library Managers

45⁰⁰

Strategic Planning and Management
for Library Managers

Joseph R. Matthews

LIBRARIES
UNLIMITED
A Member of the Greenwood Publishing Group

Westport, Connecticut • London

Library of Congress Cataloging-in-Publication Data

Matthews, Joseph R.
  Strategic planning and management for library managers / Joseph R. Matthews.
    p. cm.
  Includes bibliographical references and index.
  ISBN 1-59158-231-8 (pbk. : alk. paper)
  1. Library administration. 2. Library planning. 3. Strategic planning. I. Title.
Z678.M38 2005
025.1—dc22 2005010099

British Library Cataloguing in Publication Data is available.

Library of Congress Catalog Card Number: 2005010099
ISBN: 1–59158–231–8

First published in 2005

Libraries Unlimited, 88 Post Road West, Westport, CT 06881
A Member of the Greenwood Publishing Group, Inc.
www.lu.com

Printed in the United States of America

∞™

The paper used in this book complies with the
Permanent Paper Standard issued by the National
Information Standards Organization (Z39.48-1984).

10 9 8 7 6 5 4 3 2 1

To Dad—
Thanks for everything!

Contents

Introduction xi

Part 1: Strategies

Chapter 1—What Are Strategies? 3
    The Realities and Limits of Strategies 6
    Notes 8

Chapter 2—The Need for Strategies 11
    Setting Direction 12
    The Mission 13
    Values 19
    The Vision 21
    Strategies 24
    Summary 26
    Notes 27

Chapter 3—Schools of Strategic Thought 29
    The Design School—Strategy Formation as a Process of
        Conception 30
    The Planning School—Strategy Formation as a Formal Process 31
    The Positioning School—Strategy Formation as an Analytical
        Process 33
    The Entrepreneurial School—Strategy Formation as a Visionary
        Process 35
    The Cognitive School—Strategy Formation as a Mental Process 36
    The Learning School—Strategy Formation as an Emergent
        Process 36
    The Power School—Strategy Formation as a Process of
        Negotiation 37
    The Cultural School—Strategy Formation as a Collective
        Process 38
    The Environmental School—Strategy Formation as a Reactive
        Process 39
    The Configuration School—Strategy Formation as a Process of
        Transformation 40
    Notes 40

Chapter 4—Types of Strategies 43
    Operational Excellence 44
    Innovative Services 45
    Customer Intimacy 45

Strategic Options 46
    Focus. 47
    Differentiation 47
    Service/Product Usage 50
    Synergy. 50
Notes. 52

Part 2: Strategic Planning

Chapter 5—What Is Strategic Planning?. 57
   Notes. 60

Chapter 6—Value of Strategic Planning 61
   Notes. 64

Chapter 7—Strategic Planning Process Options. 65
   Introduction 65
   Planning Alternatives 67
     SWOT. 67
     Scenario Planning. 71
     Game Theory 73
     Decision Analysis. 74
     System Dynamic Models 76
   Strategy Formulation 76
   Setting Goals and Objectives 77
   Critical Success Factors 78
   The Plan 79
   Caveat Emptor 80
   Notes. 81

Chapter 8—Implementation 83
   Starting the Planning Process 86
   Who Should Be Involved 86
   What Is Required 88
   How 89
   Notes. 91

Part 3: Monitoring and Updating Strategies

Chapter 9—A Culture of Assessment. 95
   Listening to the Voice of the Customer 100
   Listening to the Voice of Library Staff Members 101
   Listening to the Voice of the Process. 102

Listening to the Voice of the Organization 103
Notes.. 105
Chapter 10—Tools for Managing the Library 109
Performance Measures 111
The Balanced Scorecard...................................... 123
A Library Scorecard 129
Performance Prism 130
Three Rs of Performance 132
Summary... 134
Notes.. 136

Appendix A: Sample Library Strategic Plans................... 139
Appendix B: Critique of a Library Strategic Plan 141
Index.. 145

Introduction

Ever since Donald Riggs's *Strategic Planning for Library Managers*, the library literature has paid little attention to the topic of strategic management and strategic planning.[1] Yet the importance of strategies and the vital role that strategies play within any library cannot be overstated. The purpose of this book is to explore strategies, demystify some of the persistent false impressions about strategies, identify broad categories of strategies that a library may wish to employ, discuss the role of strategies in planning and the delivery of library services, and identify some new ways in which to communicate the impact of the library' strategies on the lives of its customers.

Since the introduction of the Internet, public, academic, school, government, research and special libraries have moved into a significant activity that revolves around the topic of how to integrate the delivery of digital library services into the more traditional library services. Thus, the task that these libraries are engaged in is not the invention of a virtual library but rather they are involved in the process of re-inventing an esteemed organization.

At some point during the last 20 years most libraries moved from a focus on the growth of their collections to recognition that the most dominant force driving the library was change. No longer able to rely on the status quo of providing traditional library services, the library was confronted with a number of forces that were forcing it to adapt or cease being relevant in the lives of its customers. Yet for a great many libraries the reality of the need for change is ignored and it is business as usual. The library continues to operate using a set of policies that are the result of traditions, beliefs, rules, and unchallenged assumptions. This is a classic case of "let's stick our heads in the sand" so the library can ignore the fact that it is losing its relevance in the life of its customers.

Thomas Kuhn's notion of a paradigm shift has been applied not only in the scientific arena but also in a variety of social settings and subject disciplines, including libraries.[2] Yet as Charles Lowry has noted, the paradigm shift is not in libraries but is to be found in the organization and delivery of information.[3] Given this shift, it is incumbent upon libraries to reexamine their existing strategies for delivering information to their customers to ensure that the needs of their customers are being met. Such a reexamination requires some strategic planning as well as the need to restructure a library's policies and procedures.

> *Businesses are nothing more or less than organizations of people trying to get to a jointly defined future.*
>
> —Howard H. Stevenson[4]

Organization of the Book

This book is divided into three broad parts:

- What a strategy is and the need for strategies
- The value of and available options for strategic planning
- The need to monitor and update strategies

This book provides a compendium of useful information about the literature concerning strategies and how to effectively engage in strategic planning and management. The intent is to integrate this information into a set of tools that will assist any librarian, library board member, or funding decision maker.

Part 1: Strategies

Chapter 1: What Are Strategies?

Defining what a strategy is and its potential contribution to an organization is not as simple a task as it first might appear. Rather, a strategy can have multiple meanings depending upon the context and your perspective. This "multiple personality" tendency of strategies has led to a wide misuse of the word and how strategies are potentially applied within a library.

Chapter 2: The Need for Strategies

This chapter suggests that strategies should be developed after the library has crafted its mission statement, a statement of values, and its vision. Comparing where the library currently is with its vision will identify a gap. Filling in the gap can be done in a variety of ways (these ways are called strategies). It is important for the library to carefully consider how to best meet the needs of its customers by providing additional value to the services that it provides.

Chapter 3: Schools of Strategic Thought

When examining the strategic planning and strategic management literature over the last 30 to 40 years, it is possible to identify 10 distinct points of view. These points of view or perspectives are called schools. Each school is described and its strengths and limitations noted.

Chapter 4: Types of Strategies

Fortunately, there are a number of broad types of strategies, and within a broad category, a number of specific strategies can be chosen by the library as it moves to fill in its service gaps and move toward its vision of the future. Each specific strategy is presented and discussed to assist a library in determining if the strategy might be applicable to a specific library setting.

Part 2: Strategic Planning

Chapter 5: What Is Strategic Planning?

This chapter discusses the differences between strategic planning, which takes a broader view, and more traditional long-range planning practiced by a great many libraries.

Chapter 6: Value of Strategic Planning

The benefits that a library may derive from engaging in strategic planning are many. Which benefits and the value of those benefits will, of course, depend on the unique circumstances that exist both within the library itself and in the larger organizational context.

Chapter 7: Strategic Planning Process Options

Fortunately there are a variety of ways in which a library can go about preparing a strategic plan. Each of these approaches is identified and its strengths and limitations discussed.

Chapter 8: Implementation

For the library director or library board, the very important issues of whom to involve, what approach should be employed, and how the plan should be prepared must first be addressed.

Part 3: Monitoring and Updating Strategies

Chapter 9: A Culture of Assessment

One important aspect of developing a strategic plan is determining what performance measures to use to determine what progress is being made to achieve the objectives of the strategic plan. In other words, what performance measures will actually measure the impacts of the set of strategies chosen by the library? Part of the challenge is to involve all library staff members in the process of assessment and to make assessment a routine part of the daily activities of the library. This involvement is called a "culture of assessment."

Chapter 10: Tools for Managing the Library

The challenge for any library is to manage the resources that it is given to provide services. The library requests funds using a budget; once adopted, the budget then becomes a tool for management to control the library's operations. It is possible to combine the uses of performance measures and the library's budget, but for the most part these attempts have not met with much success. The challenge for the library's top management team is to identify an effective way to communicate the value of the library to its various stakeholders. This chapter suggests the use of three possible "balanced scorecards" as a demonstrated method for communicating with stakeholders, especially funding decision makers.

Appendixes

Appendix A provides a list of sample strategic plans for all types of libraries. Each of the plans may be accessed via the Internet. Appendix B provides an actual library strategic plan (with all identity removed to protect the innocent), along with a critique of some of the problems with this particular plan.

Notes

1. Donald E. Riggs. *Strategic Planning for Library Managers*. Phoenix, AZ: Oryx Press, 1984.

2. Thomas S. Kuhn. *The Structure of Scientific Revolutions*. Chicago: University of Chicago Press, 1962.

3. Charles B. Lowry. When's This Paradigm Shift Ending? *portal: Libraries and the Academy*, 2 (3), 2002, vii–xiii.

4. Quoted in Eileen C. Shapiro. *The Seven Deadly Sins of Business: Freeing the Corporate Mind Into Doom-Loop Thinking*. Oxford, UK: Capstone, 1998, 21.

Part 1

Strategies

Chapter 1

What Are Strategies?

Think of strategy as a bridge; values are the bedrock on which the piers of the bridge are planted, the near bank is today's reality, the far bank is the vision. Your strategy is the bridge itself.—Gordon R. Sullivan[1]

The word *strategy* is military in nature and is derived from the Greek word "strategos"—which refers both to an army (military force as an instrument of the state) and to a general or the commander-in-chief who is directing the movements and operations of a campaign (application of military force).[2] One of the earliest known military strategists was Sun Tzu, a Chinese military officer who lived in the sixth century BC. He wrote *The Art of War*, an influential book on military tactics. Sun Tzu's strategies have been adapted to today's business environment in a recent book.[3]

Reflect for a moment about the different strategies employed by the two opposing armies at Concord during the Revolutionary War. The British employed the traditional strategy of dressing their soldiers in colorful red uniforms and marching them in rows against the enemy. Meanwhile, the rag-tag, non-uniformed Americans were assuming positions among the trees and rocks, taking a few shots and then falling back to fire again and again. The Americans were using an unusual and ultimately more successful strategy of conserving their assets while inflicting real damage on the British troops.

If you don't like change, you're going to like irrelevance even less.
—General Eric Shinseki, U.S. Army[4]

> *No advantage and no success is ever permanent.*
> *The winners are those who keep moving.*
> —Michael Dell[5]

Strategies, strategic planning, and strategic management have been successfully applied to all types of nonmilitary organizations, including libraries, and having a better understanding of these topics can be helpful to any library. Strategies and strategic planning have been variously defined as follows:

> Top management's plans to attain outcomes consistent with the organization's missions and goals.[6]

> A continuous process of making present entrepreneurial (risk-taking) decisions systematically and with the greatest knowledge of their futurity; organizing systematically the efforts needed to carry out their decisions; and measuring the results of these decisions against the expectations through organized feedback.[7]

> Strategic planning is the process of deciding on objectives of the organization, on changes in these objectives, on the resources used to attain these objectives, and on the policies that are to govern the acquisition, use, and disposition of these resources.[8]

> Strategy is the creation of a unique and valuable position, involving a different set of activities.[9]

> Strategy may be thought of as a pattern of purposes, policies, programs, actions, decisions, and/or resource allocations that defines what an organization is, what it does, and why it does it.[10]

Given the plethora of books and articles about strategies, strategic planning, and strategic management, it is possible to continue in a similar vein indefinitely. Most business schools devote more than one class to strategic management. Yet despite efforts to develop a single definition for strategy, it is more realistic to consider multiple definitions.

Ask any group of people to define strategy, and the most likely first response will be that strategy is a *plan*—a guide for future action or a means to get from point A to point B.[11] In this definition, strategy is the intended outcome or destination. However, asking these same individuals to articulate the actual strategy pursued over the past few years by the organizations that they work for will, in some cases, reveal that there is a difference between the written strategies and the actual strategies being employed.

Thus, strategy is also consistency in behavior over time—a *pattern*. Looking back at the strategies actually used by an organization is another way of defining strategy as *realized*. The decisions made by an organization, one by one, over the course of time, may lead to consistency or a pattern.

Yet few strategies are purely deliberate (no learning takes place within the organization), just as few strategies are purely emergent (no control exists within the organization). All real-world strategies are some combination of these two extremes: The organization is able to exercise some control while fostering learning.

It should be abundantly clear to even a casual observer that intended strategies are not always realized. As observed in later chapters, there are many reasons why lack of implementation happens in an organization. Of interest is the fact that some companies and their CEOs have failed due to bad execution of strategy rather than bad strategy per se.[12]

Some observers, most notably Michael Porter, who is acknowledged to be one of the world's strategy gurus, consider that a strategy is a *position*—the organization is able to place a specific product or a service in a particular market. In this view, strategy is looking out to the external marketplace. On the other hand, some believe that strategy is a *perspective,* or how an organization has historically delivered a product or service. These latter individuals are looking up to see the "big picture." Not surprisingly, it is often necessary to use both definitions—position and perspective—to define strategy.

Another frequently encountered definition of strategy is that it is a *ploy,* a maneuver to counter or outwit the actions of a competitor. Here the strategy is the threat of an action rather than an actual activity.

When all of the definitions and perspectives are boiled down, strategies are really concerned with one fundamental question: how? Organizational strategies concern how to grow the organization, how to satisfy customers, how to overcome the pressures of competitors, how to respond to changing market conditions, and how to manage the organization and develop needed organizational capabilities. The how's of strategy tend to be specific, customized to meet each organization's situation and objectives.

U.S. Army Strategies

The U.S. Army has developed nine fundamental strategies that have proven effective over time:[13]

- *The Objective:* The objective or purpose in battle is to direct all efforts toward a decisive, obtainable goal.

- *Simplicity:* Prepare uncomplicated plans and concise orders to ensure thorough understanding and execution.

- *Unity of Command:* For every task there should be unity of effort under one responsible commander.

- *The Offensive:* Seize, retain, and exploit the initiative.

- *Maneuver.* Position your resources to favor the accomplishment of your mission.

- *Mass:* Achieve superiority at the decisive time and place.

- *Economy of Force:* Allocate to secondary efforts minimum essential combat power.

- *Surprise:* Accomplish your purpose before the enemy can effectively react.

- *Security:* Never permit the enemy to acquire an unpredicted advantage.

Effective management always means asking the right questions.

—Robert Heller[14]

The Realities and Limits of Strategies

After only a brief consideration of strategy, it becomes fairly clear that strategy is a two-edged sword. For every strength there is a corresponding drawback or weakness. Consider the following:

1. **Strategy defines the organization.**

   Strength: A clearly articulated strategy provides staff members with a way to understand their organization and ways to distinguish it from others. Strategy means performing *different* activities than do rivals or performing similar activities in *different* ways. Strategy provides a convenient way to comprehend what the organization does.

Limitation: Defining an organization, especially with stereotypes, means that the rich complexity of the facilities, staff, and procedures are not appreciated.

2. **Strategy sets direction.**

Strength: The primary role of strategy is to identify how the organization will achieve its goals.

Limitation: A strategy can also induce a set of limitations, similar to blinders, that will mask potential problems as well as cause an organization to ignore other potentially better strategies. And although direction is very important, determining the appropriate speed of implementation is equally so.

3. **Strategy focuses effort.**

Strength: Strategy will promote the coordination of activities and special projects. Having a clear goal helps encourage staff members to move in the same direction.

Limitation: An organization ceases to be open to other opportunities that may arise during the course of the year. A new or revised strategy may deliver the products and services in ways that an organization's customers will be very excited about.

4. **Strategy provides consistency.**

Strength: Strategy is a way to simplify and explain how the organization will interact with its customers and the outside environment.

Limitation: Inconsistencies and problems can be the cause of few creative solutions that would deliver more value to an organization's customers. Since a strategy is not a reality but rather a representation of reality, it can have a distorting effect.

> *A foolish consistency is the hobgoblin of little minds.*
> —Ralph Waldo Emerson[15]

To develop successful strategies, an organization must simultaneously carefully plan and act upon opportunities, have a broad vision and focus on details, and establish direction from the top but also embrace participation from all levels within the organization. Or, as observed by F. Scott Fitzgerald: "The test of a first-rate intelligence is the ability to hold two opposed ideas in the mind at the same time and still retain the ability to function."[16] To successfully consider and implement a series of strategies means that a librarian will need to understand, hold, and synthesize various opposing views, and one of the most important views that must be retained during any planning activity that leads to a set of strategies is how to create value for the customer.

Notes

1. Quoted in William A. Schiemann and John H. Lingle. *Bullseye! Hitting Your Strategic Targets Through High-Impact Measurement*. New York: Free Press, 1999, 61.

2. *The Oxford English Dictionary*, Volume 10. Oxford: The Clarendon Press, 1989, 852.

3. D. G. Krause. *Sun Tzu: The Art of War for Executives*. London: Nicholas Brealey, 1996.

4. Quoted in Tom Peters. *Re-imagine!* New York: DK, 2003, title page.

5. Quoted in Kathleen M. Eisenhardt. Strategy as Strategic Decision Making. *Sloan Management Review*, 40 (3), Spring 1999, 66.

6. P. Wright, C. Pringle, and M. Kroll. *Strategic Management Text and Cases*. Needham Heights, MA: Allyn and Bacon, 1992, 3.

7. Peter F. Drucker. *Management: Tasks, Responsibilities and Practice*. New York: Harper & Row, 1973, 125.

8. Robert N. Anthony. *Management Control Systems*. Homewood, IL: Richard D. Irwin, 1965, 4.

9. Michael Porter. What Is Strategy. *Harvard Business Review*, 74 (6), November–December 1996, 61–78.

10. Cynthia Dereli. Strategy and Strategic Decision-Making in the Smaller Local Authority. *International Journal of Public Sector Management*, 16 (4), 2003, 25–60.

11. Henry Mintzberg. The Strategic Concept 1: Five Ps for Strategy. *California Management Review*, 30 (1), June 1987, 11–24.

12. R. Charan and G. Colvin. Why CEOs Fail. *Fortune*, 139, June 21, 1999, 68–78. A similar analysis performed in the early 1980s noted the same result. See Walter Kiechel. Corporate Strategists Under Fire. *Fortune*, 106, December 27, 1982, 34–39.

13. *US Army Field Service Regulations, Operations*. Washington, DC: U.S. Army, 2003.

14. Quoted in Andy Neely, Chris Adams, and Mike Kennerley. *The Performance Prism: The Scorecard for Measuring and Managing Business Success.* London: Prentice Hall, 2002, 344.

15. *Essays: Self-Reliance.* 1841. Republished: New York: Dover, 1993.

16. "Crackup," 1936, cited in *Bartlett's Familiar Quotations,* 16th ed. Justin Kaplan, general editor. Boston: Little, Brown, 1992.

Chapter 2

The Need for Strategies

Courage is sustained by calling up a vision of the goal.
—A. G. Sertillanges[1]

All organizations have a plan. It may be called a business plan, a strategic plan, a long-range plan, or one of many other labels. The plan may not be in written form, or it may be a bound, impressive document. The plan may be known to only a few people or be shared widely with employees, suppliers, and customers. It may be arbitrary or systematic.

The key to understanding an organization's plan is to see how the most precious resources within the organization (including such things as money and people's time) are allocated and used to deliver products and services. Within many organizations, including libraries, a goal may be articulated but because there is no change in the way resources are applied, staff quickly realize that the goal is not important and that maintaining the status quo is all that is expected.

The first purpose of any planning process is to identify the library's customers and how the library will provide products and services that will be of value to these customers. The second part of the plan should identify what capabilities the library needs (sometimes these capabilities are called "critical success factors") to be successful.

A well-constructed plan can provide a road map to success and assist in informing all staff members how they can contribute to the results. A good strategic plan is likely to have most, if not all, of the following components:

- A succinct and understandable mission statement

- A clear focus on how specific customers are to be served

- A vision of what the future will be like

11

- An explicit statement of the strategic initiatives or focus the library will undertake

- Specific objectives that will support the strategic initiatives

- Organizational values and culture that will support the implementation of the chosen strategy

- The choice of specific performance measures that will inform the decision makers of the progress being made to achieve the vision.

The unfortunate reality is that most plans, despite their titles, are voluminous "dust collectors." A shorter and more precise plan that sets the direction for the entire library is a much better objective for the planning process. A clear set of strategies for competing in an increasingly complex world will result in a concentrated focus that can be easily summarized and communicated throughout the organization. Organizations with effective plans follow the planning rule of "decisions, not descriptions," while others seem to follow "descriptions, not decision."

The primary purposes of any planning process, regardless of what it is called, are to set direction, develop plans and strategies, and monitor progress, as shown in Figure 2.1.

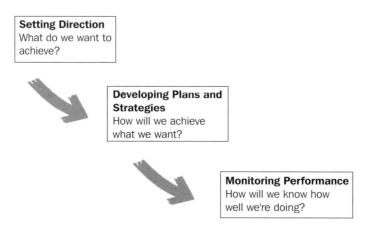

Figure 2.1. Aligning Mission, Vision, Strategies, and Measurement

Setting Direction

The primary role of top management is to set the direction for the library. This can be best accomplished and communicated to the stakeholders through the development of a strategic plan. Among the topics that should be addressed in such a plan are the following:

- *Mission:* The raison d'être for the library. Why does the library exist? Whom does the library serve?

- *Values:* The basic beliefs that the library is founded upon. Values rarely change because they reflect something that is viewed as important or almost sacred.

- *Vision:* Usually prepared by top management with the involvement of many others, it focuses on what the library will be like in 10 to 20 years (time horizon may vary).

- *Strategic Focus:* The key thing that will differentiate the library from its competitors. Although many individuals may be involved in the development of the strategies, ultimately top management is responsible for their selection and implementation.

- *Critical Success Factors:* The important things that the library must do well to overcome today's problems, assist in meeting and exceeding the competition, and help the library achieve its vision.

These concepts are at the core of an effective library—informing and inspiring all stakeholders, guiding decisions, and aligning the actions of all staff members (see Figure 2.2).

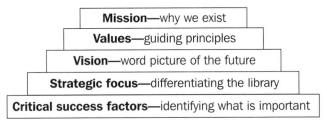

Figure 2.2. Core Concepts of the Planning Process

The Mission

The typical mission statement is a long, awkward sentence [paragraph, or page] that demonstrates management's inability to think clearly.
—Scott Adams[2]

Some organizations call the mission statement their "purpose statement" or the organization's central reason for existing. Your organization's mission statement should address the following questions: Whom do you serve? What roles do you play in the lives of your customers? What are you trying to accomplish?

An organization's mission statement should describe its present activities ("who we are and what do we do"). A good library mission statement includes a focus on the customer's served by the library, an indication of the products and services provided, and how the customers benefit.

Public, academic, government, and some research libraries do not, of course, share the profit imperative, as is the case with a great many special libraries. The success of the former libraries is often dependent upon the development of a crystallizing mission statement. One research study found that a clear mission statement was one of four primary characteristics of successful nonprofit organizations.[3] The value of a powerful mission statement is that it can energize employees, reduce the need for supervision, and assist in making decisions within the organization. As David Osborne and Ted Gaebler noted in *Reinventing Government*:

> The experience of hashing out the fundamental purpose of an organization—debating all the different assumptions and views held by its members and agreeing on one basic mission—can be a powerful one. When it is done right, a mission statement can drive an entire organization from top to bottom.[4]

If a library's mission statement not only sets a clear definition of "who we are and what do we do" but also indicates where the organization is headed, then it has combined the concepts of a mission statement and strategic vision or a vision statement into a single statement describing both where it is now and where it is going. However, it is important to distinguish between the library's mission and strategic vision.

It is crucial that the library's mission be clear so that all stakeholders have an understanding of the goals and direction of the organization. A mission statement should

- define what the library does and does not do,
- distinguish that organization from the competition,
- specify the library's customers,
- identify the benefits from using the library,
- focus on the present (not be a future-focused vision statement),
- create a shared understanding of the purpose of the library,
- be brief (Challenge: Can you state your library's mission statement in one sentence?), and
- be clearly written and employ no buzzwords.

Peter Drucker, the renowned teacher, author, and consultant, has observed that some organizations make the mistake of turning their mission statement into "hero sandwiches of good intentions."[5] He has further noted that purpose and mission are the foundation upon which an organization's plans and strategies are built:

> Only a clear definition of the mission and purpose of the business makes possible clear and realistic business objectives. It is the foundation for priorities, strategies, plans, and work assignments. It is the starting point for the design of managerial jobs, and above all, for the design of managerial structures. Structure follows strategy. Strategy determines what the key activities are in a given business. And strategy requires knowing "what our business is and what it should be."[6]

Most library mission statements are simply too long, list activities, fail to identify a greater good, often employ library jargon, and, as a result, are not very memorable. Suggestions for developing or improving your library's mission statement include the following:

- The "5 Whys"—Start with a simple descriptive statement such as, "We provide X services." Then ask, "Why is this important?" five times.[7] With each iteration of the question, the true mission of the library will begin to emerge so that the value or contribution of the library in the lives of its customer becomes clear. This helps everyone step back from the typical micro view of the library to discover the bigger issues that define the library.

- Gast's Laws—Respond to six questions based on principles developed by Walter Gast:[8]

  1. What "want-satisfying" service do we provide and constantly seek to improve?

  2. How do we increase the quality of life for our customers and stakeholders?

  3. How do we provide opportunities to productively employ people?

  4. How do we create a high-quality work experience for our employees?

  5. How do we live up to the obligations to provide just wages?

  6. How do we fulfill the obligation of providing a return on the financial and human resources we expend?

A number of benefits arise from clarifying and agreeing on the library's mission. Principally, an excellent mission statement will foster a habit of focusing discussion on what is really important. One of the realities for almost all libraries is that the individuals and boards responsible for the library do not dedicate much time to discussing important topics but rather seem to spend their time when they do meet on announcements, updates, and trivial matters.

Clarity of organizational purpose will help the library's top management team become better leaders. Such clarity can assist the organization in understanding which rules help control conflict and which may need to be changed. The mission statement can also assist individuals in disconnecting the means from the end so that the discussion is about what problems to solve rather than about solutions. David Osborne and Ted Gaebler suggest that if governments stick to *steering* (purpose and problem definition), then they are less likely to be a captive of any one approach to *rowing* (solutions).

A number of sample mission statements are included here to illustrate that good and bad statements are developed by all types of libraries. In most cases, these mission statements are too lengthy and don't really get at the heart of the library's mission. Too often these statements erroneously include processes that the library uses to deliver its mission. In other cases, the statements articulate feelings the library is attempting to engender in the lives of its customers. The goal is a succinct statement about what the library does—it's best if the statement could be printed on a T-shirt!

Sample Mission Statements

Academic Libraries

Brigham Young University: The mission of the Harold B. Lee Library is to support learning, teaching, and research at BYU by:

- Serving as a center of learning by providing a place for students and faculty to actively engage in study and research;

- Selecting, acquiring, organizing, preserving, and providing access to scholarly information related to the university's curriculum and research programs;

- Extending access to library resources and services through the use of technology;

- Engaging students and faculty in finding and using scholarly information; and

- Supporting life-long learning.

Within available resources, services are also extended to other Church libraries, members of the Church, and local community members. As a research library, the Harold B. Lee Library participates and partners with local, regional, national, and international academic library consortia.

UCLA: The mission of the University Library is to provide access to and delivery of information resources to UCLA faculty, students, and staff in support of the research and instructional mission of the university. The Library develops, organizes, and preserves collections for optimal use and provides links to remote information sources. The Library provides services, including instruction for information literacy and information management, to enable its users to fulfill their academic and intellectual needs. The Library provides resources and services to non-UCLA users to the extent possible.

Relying on its highly skilled staff, the Library encourages innovation, capitalizes on appropriate technologies, forges effective partnerships, and aggressively promotes excellence.

Duke University: In active support of Duke University's mission: we provide to the University and wider academic community a place for self-education and discovery; we promote scholarship and good citizenship through information literacy; we acquire, organize, preserve, and deliver information resources and assist users in their effective use; we create a great library for a great University.

Public Libraries

St. Joseph County Public Library Mission Statement

- We provide expert training and instruction so that you can use the latest technology to find what you need.

- We provide easy access to the most wanted and needed library materials of all types so you can reach your goals and satisfy your whims.

- We provide a community gathering place to learn, to meet neighbors, to make new friends, and to have fun.

- Whatever information you want, wherever it is, SJCPL, the **Best** public library anywhere, will find it.

The mission of the *San Diego Public Library* is to:

Respond to the information needs of San Diego's diverse communities.

Ensure equal access to local, national, and global resources.

Anticipate and address the educational, cultural, business, and recreational interests of the public.

Develop and provide welcoming environments.

Multnomah County Library serves the people of Multnomah County by providing books and other materials to meet their informational, educational, cultural, and recreational needs.

The Cuyahoga County Public Library will provide our communities free and open access to information, giving every person the opportunity for enrichment, inspiration, and entertainment.

The Naperville Public Libraries mission is to make a positive difference in the community by providing excellence in library service.

The mission of the *Medina County District Library* is to enhance the quality of life in Medina County by providing the resources and services necessary to satisfy the evolving informational needs and recreational pursuits of the community.

The *Santa Clara County Library* is an open forum promoting knowledge, ideas, and cultural enrichment. The library provides free access to informational, educational, and recreational materials and services. In response to community needs, the library provides diverse resources on a wide variety of subjects and viewpoints and helps people use these resources.

The mission of the *Richland County Free Library (SC)* is meeting our citizens' needs for reading, learning, and information.

The *Kitchener Public Library* is both a resource and a gateway, connecting our community with the sources of information and the works of imagination it needs and enjoys . . .

by identifying and fulfilling the community's needs

by embracing new outlooks and opportunities

by creating partnerships with our community

by cultivating our greatest resource, our staff.

Special Libraries

Company X: To promptly provide quality technical, business, and marketplace information to individuals and groups within the company at a competitive cost.

National Institute of Standards and Technology (NIST). The NIST Virtual Library . . . where our customers' needs shape our future.

Grossmont Healthcare. The Herrick Library is a digital library designed to provide this information through print and non-print resources, including books, journals, pamphlets, videotapes, electronic media, and online computer databases. The staff is trained to help users find materials to satisfy their health information needs.

Values

Values are the guiding principles and the deeply ingrained operating rules of an organization. They represent the ways things get done in an organization. These beliefs or enduring principles influence the attitudes and behavior of a library's employees. Exciting and dynamic organizations, including some libraries, have a value statement that clearly articulates

- the value of the customer,
- the importance of staff members,
- how things are accomplished,
- the importance of efficiency,
- the type of communication that is valued, and
- the role of performance measures.

Values represent the deeply held beliefs within the organization and are demonstrated by the day-to-day behaviors of all staff members. These are the principles that guide an organization in its conduct and its relationships. Having a concise and compelling statement of values helps staff understand what they can do to assist the library in achieving its vision. In some cases, a library will articulate its values using a written statement called a customer's "Bill of Rights."

Having an articulated set of values will assist the library in recruiting individuals who have similar values, aid in motivating staff members, support the process of implementing changes within the library, and act as a guide in the event emergencies should arise.

Frequently used terms that articulate an organization's values include *integrity, openness, courtesy, respect, accountability,* and *responsibility.* The goal is to go beyond listing values to crafting a set of values that are meaningful to the library's staff members and customers.

Although a written set of values is helpful, there is a danger that the espoused values are not the values being followed by staff members on a day-to-day basis. Should this occur, the library's management team would likely be perceived as hypocritical. Clearly every organization has a set of values that are in operation today. Understanding the current value system forms the foundation for changing values in the future. Richard Barrett, in *Liberating the Corporate Soul,* created a "value audit instrument" can be used to discover personal values, organizational values, and ideal organizational values.[9] Using this or a similar instrument, organizations are able to discover the degree of alignment between personal and organizational values and culture.

In addition, it may be helpful to respond to the following set of questions about core values, developed by Jim Collins:[10]

- How would you describe to your loved ones the core values you stand for in your work and that you hope they stand for in their working lives?

- If you awoke tomorrow morning with enough money to retire for the rest of your life, would you continue to hold on to these core values?

- Perhaps more important, can you envision these values being as valid 100 years from now as they are today?

- What core values do you bring to work—values you hold to be so fundamental that you would hold them regardless of whether or not they were rewarded?

- Would you want the organization to continue to hold these values even if, at some point, one or more of them became a competitive disadvantage?

- If you were to start a new organization tomorrow in a different line of work, what core values would you build into the new organization regardless of its activities?

One of the important challenges facing librarians as they strive to define their values is to recognize the gap that exists between those who see themselves as personal custodians and institutional guardians of received library values and others who believe librarians should be working to create value for library customers. At one end of the spectrum are those who view their purpose as more to comfort, advocate for, and defend libraries rather than to embrace values that focus on providing value to customers:

[Being] valuable is not about our professional values; in the paradigm of the value of . . . libraries we are the producers, not the customers of our services. Our personal sense of what is valuable doesn't matter unless it matches that of our customers.[11]

Michael Gorman is a vocal advocate for maintaining the traditional library values of stewardship, service, intellectual freedom, rationalism, literacy and learning, equity of access to recorded knowledge and information, privacy, and democracy.[12] Alternatively, Gary Deane has suggested that a "value gap" exists in many libraries and that libraries should focus on customer value and the means of delivering it.[13]

In assessing your library's values, consider whether

- there is an explicit statement of values,

- the values are clear and consistent,

- the values reflect how the library conducts its business,

- staff members endorse and embrace the values with enthusiasm, and

- espoused values reflect actual values.

Clearly, values support the mission of the library and help achieve organizational objectives. Having a vision statement and a written set of values provides awareness of where you are (and have come from) and where you are heading. Having a specific destination allows the library to focus rather than attempting to be all things to all people.

The Vision

Vision comes from the heart, not the head. Our purpose in creating the vision is to clarify what we wish to create, knowing all along that we may never get there.

—Peter Block[14]

Few, if any, forces in human affairs are as powerful as shared vision.

—Peter Senge[15]

A good vision statement is clear, memorable, motivating, and customer-related, and its goals or targets can be translated into actions that can be measured. The vision statement sets out long-term targets and success criteria for the library and acts as a focus for identifying the key strategic activities that must be accomplished if the vision is to be achieved.[16] Thus, a vision statement can be thought of as a coherent and powerful statement of what the library can and should be (five) years hence (the time frame will vary, depending upon the type of library and other outside influences).

If a vision statement is too long, it will fail to be memorable. An inspiring vision

- invigorates and challenges,

- is an important ingredient for change,

- will positively affect the behaviors of staff members,

- is the standard against which all decisions are made, and

- will almost dictate the choice of performance measures that will be used to measure progress.

Unless the vision is focused on meeting customer needs, the reason for the library's existence is being ignored:

> Vision translates mission into truly meaningful intended results —and guides the allocation of time, energy, and resources. In my experience, it is only through a compelling vision that a deep sense of purpose comes alive.[17]

It is important to look beyond today and think strategically about (1) the impact of new technologies available now and in the near future, (2) how customer needs and expectations are changing, (3) the consequences of engaging or ignoring the realities of competitors, and (4) the other external and internal factors that drive what the library needs to be doing to prepare for the future. Armed with a clear and compelling strategic vision, managers and other staff members have a compass to guide resource allocation and a basis for crafting strategy to get the library where it needs to go.

> *If you do not know where you're heading, you're likely to end up somewhere else.*
>
> —Yogi Berra[18]

As a part of the process to identify and create a vision, the library should consider that it could be viewed in a variety of ways, among the more noteworthy of which are the following:

- *As a physical collection:* A collection of materials with a variety of formats—books, journals, audiovisual, microforms, documents, maps, and so forth.

- *As nurturing the independent learner:* Providing support for independent learners, particularly individuals interested in expanding their horizons.

- *As a knowledge navigator:* In addition to providing traditional in-library reference service, also providing an online 24/7 reference service. This can be complemented by providing and updating a variety of pathfinders.

- *As a source of information technology:* Providing access to information and computer technology as well as staff with superior information management skills.

- *As an information provider:* Providing access to its collection and skilled professional librarians to assist users in meeting their information needs. In some cases, the library focuses on collecting and organizing information about topics that would be of interest to those served by the library.

- *As a document deliverer:* Delivering documents, in particular copies of journal articles, using interlibrary loan and links to document delivery firms.

- *As a researcher:* Skilled librarians providing their research skills to customers of the library.

- *As a meeting place:* Providing access to meeting rooms of varying sizes.

- *As a source of information literacy:* Assisting in developing information management or information literacy skills.

- *As the "preferred" information intermediary known for providing access to quality information resources (physical and electronic resources):* As the library moves toward providing more electronic resources it becomes more of an "invisible" intermediary, sometimes called a portal.

- *As a memory institution:* Preserving materials of value to the library's customers may be important for some libraries.

Joel Finlay has suggested a brainstorming process that can assist a library in developing a vision of the future that will be compelling.[19] An effective vision for any organization will

- fit the organization and the times,

- set an ambitious standard of excellence (define a key criterion for success),

- clarify direction and purpose (future focus),

- drive strategy,

- evoke the unique competence of the organization to create competitive advantage,

- emphasize the importance of service and technology,

- stimulate and inspire enthusiasm and commitment,

- be clear and easy to understand, and

- facilitate cooperation and collaboration.

Organizations with winning vision statements are able to express an energizing view of the future in terms of customer benefits. Although the goals may be aggressive, they are achievable with some effort. Unfortunately, more than half of all libraries do not have a vision statement. It's as if "more of the same" is assumed to be just fine.

> *A vision without a plan is a hallucination.*
> —Anonymous

One of the real challenges for any organization that attempts to implement change to achieve its vision is that the dream often becomes a nightmare, for the following reasons:

- *Fear*—The organization may not want to break out of its traditional comfort zone or is held back by the problems experienced with prior programs that involved a significant amount of change.

- *Fatigue*—The organization is tired and unwilling to make decisions or makes the wrong decisions based on reluctance to move forward.

- *Frustration*—Lack of cooperation within an organization can lead to conflicting emotions and no real progress toward achieving the vision.

- *Failure*—Failure can occur if the vision is not imaginative and was developed without staff at all levels having an opportunity to assist in the development and review of the vision statement.

Strategies

As a strategy for crossing a river the organization might decide to erect a pontoon bridge, a cantilever bridge, a suspension bridge, a drawbridge, or a truss bridge—each a different strategy. It further might employ various tactics as to type of materials used to build the bridge, whether to build it on-site or off-site, and whether to construct it using the resources of the organization itself or using an outside contractor.

Library services have evolved over the course of time, and little thought has been given to what strategies might be employed to more effectively meet the needs of the library's customers. Initially libraries acquired, cataloged, and stored materials (this is often referred to as the "warehousing approach" or the "just in case" strategy). Access to collections migrated from closed stacks to open, which facilitated browsable searching by the library's customers. Further, as collections grew and library customers encountered problems finding the desired materials, new library services such as reference were introduced. Yet there has never been a fundamental discussion among librarians about what strategies would be most effective in a particular set of circumstances.

The attempt by some organizations to find the "right or correct" strategy—in the hope that that is what is needed—is not likely to succeed. Michael Porter, a Harvard Business School professor and well-known expert in the area of strategic planning, has noted that strategy cannot be limited to those at the top of an organization but rather must involve all staff members as they go about completing their tasks.[20] In short, implementation of a particular strategy is more important than finding the "right" strategy.

> *Successful business strategy is about actively shaping the game you play, not just playing the game you find.*
> —Adam M. Brandenburger and
> Barry J. Nalebuff[21]

As discussed in chapter 1, the management literature is replete with definitions of strategy, which fall into four categories:

- A *plan* or a means from getting from here to there.

- A *pattern* of actions over time. For example, focusing on a particular market segment.

- A *position* that reflects decisions to offer products and services in particular markets.

- A *perspective*, vision, or direction of what the organization is to become.

A strategy is a plan of action with a shared understanding designed to accomplish a specific goal that focuses on how a given objective will be achieved. Strategies are designed to move the library toward the vision of the library and to eliminate the gap that exists between where the library is today and where it wants to be tomorrow. Strategies are *not* the programmatic goals and objectives that most libraries have historically developed. For example, some libraries develop programmatic goals that can be grouped into several categories (services, technology, resources, staff development). Such an approach does not reflect a coherent set of strategies but is rather a potpourri of goals and objectives and represents a strategy known as "more of the same."

Strategies are about making choices and deliberately choosing to be different. Strategy allows an organization to create a sustainable advantage. It recognizes that it is not possible to be all things to all people and thus focuses on choices.

Ultimately, a strategy is judged by how well it delivers long-term added value for the customers of the organization. And how a library adds value is reflective of its core competencies and how well it delivers its services to meet the needs of its customers. Identifying the ways in which the library adds value and the appropriate strategies for a library to pursue is the responsibility of the management team for the library. In short, focusing on the "big picture" is much more important than the operational day-to-day crises that seem to occupy so much time of library staff members.

> *Strategies for taking the hill won't necessarily hold it.*
>
> —Amar Bhide[22]

Successful organizations have the ability to identify the four or five key areas of strategic focus, characterized by the following:

- Customers appreciate and value what the strategic focus provides.

- Resources are allocated to ensure the absolute best service is provided.

- Really excellent services are difficult for competitors to duplicate.

- Good strategies focus on what capabilities the library is really good at.

Summary

All types of successful organizations, including libraries, utilize a strategic planning process that is appropriate to them. Successful and unsuccessful organizations demonstrate the following good and poor characteristics, respectively:

Good	Poor

The Plan

Market focus	Shotgun approach
Mission	Internal focus
Vision	Lack of vision
Strategic focus	Unfocused
Strategies	"To do" list
Balanced measurements	Few performance measures

Planning Process

Customers and capabilities	Internal
Obstacles to success identified	Obstacles ignored
Communication throughout the organization	Limited communication
All levels understand strategies and plan for implementation	Crisis management

Using the Plan

Top management commitment	Inconsistent commitment
Reporting on results	Performance measures not linked to plan
Widespread sharing of the plan	Limited sharing
Plan evolves with time	Plan is ignored

Notes

1. *The Intellectual Life: Its Spirit, Conditions, Methods.* Washington, DC: Catholic University of America Press, 1987, 94.

2. Quoted in Maurice B. Line. What Do People Need of Libraries, and How Can We Find out? *Australian Academic & Research Libraries*, 27, June 1996, 79.

3. E. B. Knauft, Renee Berger, and Sandra Gray. *Profiles of Excellence.* San Francisco: Jossey-Bass, 1991.

4. David Osborne and Ted Gaebler. *Reinventing Government: How the Entre-preneurial Spirit Is Transforming the Public Sector.* Reading, MA: Addison-Wesley, 1992.

5. Peter Drucker. *Managing the Non-Profit Organization.* New York: HarperBusiness, 1990, 5.

6. Peter Drucker. *Management: Tasks, Responsibilities, Practices.* New York: Butterworth-Heinemann, 1988, 68.

7. James C. Collins and Jerry I. Porras. Building Your Company's Vision. *Harvard Business Review*, September–October 1996, 65–77.

8. Tom Krattenmaker. Write a Mission Statement That Your Company Is Willing to Live with. *Harvard Management Update*, March 2002, 5–9.

9. Richard Barrett. *Liberating the Corporate Soul*. Boston: Butterworth Heinemann, 1998.

10. Jim Collins. *Leader to Leader*. San Francisco: Jossey-Bass, 1999.

11. Eleanor Jo Rodger. Value and Vision. *American Libraries*, 33 (10), November 2002, 50.

12. Michael Gorman. Values of Steel in Thirty Days. *American Libraries*, 31 (4), April 2000, 39.

13. Gary Deane. Bridging the Value Gap: Getting Past Professional Values to Customer Value in the Public Library. *Public Libraries*, September/October 2003, 315–19.

14. Peter Block. *The Answer to How Is Yes: Acting on What Matters.* San Francisco: Berrett-Koehler, 2001, 37.

15. Peter M. Senge. *The Fifth Discipline*. New York: Doubleday, 1990, 206.

16. Nils-Goran Olve, Jan Roy, and Magnus Wetter. *Performance Drivers: A Practical Guide to Using the Balanced Scorecard.* New York: Wiley, 1999.

17. Peter Senge. The Practice of Innovation. *Leader to Leader*, 9, September 1998, 16–22.

18. Quoted at Baseball World Quote Archive. Available at: http://www.geocities.com/Colosseum/Park/1138/quotes/quotesberra.html (accessed February 26, 2005).

19. Joel S. Finlay. The Strategic Visioning Process. *Public Administration Quarterly*, 18 (1), Spring 1994, 64–74.

20. Michael Porter. What Is Strategy? *Harvard Business Review*, 74 (6), November/December 1996, 61–79.

21. Quoted in Arthur A. Thompson Jr. and A. J. Strickland III. *Crafting and Executing Strategy: Text and Readings*. New York: McGraw-Hill, 2001, 149.

22. Quoted in Thompson and Strickland, *Crafting and Executing Strategy*, 149.

Chapter 3

Schools of Strategic Thought

> *Competitive strategy is about being different. It means deliberately choosing to perform activities differently or to perform different activities than rivals to deliver a unique mix of value.*—Michael E. Porter[1]

Not surprisingly, over the last 40 years or so a number of schools of thought have developed pertaining to the topic of strategy, strategic planning, and strategic management. Although it is possible to divide the literature of a topic into any number of groups depending on inclination and perspective, 10 schools of thought about the strategy process are noted here:

1. The Design School—Strategy formation as a process of *conception*

2. The Planning School—Strategy formation as a *formal* process

3. The Positioning School—Strategy formation as an *analytical* process

4. The Entrepreneurial School—Strategy formation as a *visionary* process

5. The Cognitive School—Strategy formation as a *mental* process

6. The Learning School—Strategy formation as an *emergent* process

7. The Power School—Strategy formation as a process of *negotiation*

8. The Cultural School—Strategy formation as a *collective* process

9. The Environmental School—Strategy formation as a *reactive* process

10. The Configuration School—Strategy formation as a process of *transformation*.[2]

The first three schools are *prescriptive* in nature and focus on how strategies should be formulated. The next six schools have to do with *describing* how strategies are formulated and are less troubled with prescribing ideal strategy formulation. The last school attempts to *integrate* several schools into a process that suggests that an organization developing and using strategies moves through various stages that occur over time.

The Design School—Strategy Formation as a Process of Conception

The Design School began during the late 1950s and mid-1960s with the publication of several influential books.[3] This school places particular emphasis on an appraisal of the external environment and the internal situation using the classic SWOT analysis (Strengths, Weaknesses, Opportunities, and Threats). Also shaping strategy formulation are the values of the organization's management as well as an assessment of the organization's social responsibilities. The actual development of alternative strategies is not clearly articulated other than to note that this is a creative act.

The various strategies are then evaluated, typically using the following four criteria:

> *Advantage*: The strategy should provide for the creation and/or maintenance of a competitive advantage.
>
> *Consistency*: The strategy(ies) selected must not produce inconsistent goals and policies.
>
> *Harmony*: The strategy must acknowledge the challenges of the external environment and the culture and capabilities of the organization.
>
> *Feasibility*: The selected strategy cannot exhaust available resources nor create serous problems.[4]

Once the strategy is selected, it must then be implemented. Several basic premises underlie the Design School, as noted by Henry Mintzberg and others:[5]

> • *Strategy formation should be a deliberate process of conscious thought.* Effective strategies are the result of a carefully controlled process of thinking about the organization.

- *Responsibility for the deliberate process rests with the chief executive officer—the strategist.* This is somewhat analogous to the "command-and-control" mentality that allocates all major decisions to top management, which then enforces them on the organization.

- *Strategy formation should be kept simple and informal.* This latter requirement is somewhat difficult to meet because most SWOT analyses are the result of a formal and often lengthy process.

- *Strategies should be unique, or one of a kind.*

- *Strategies are complete when they are fully formulated.* The strategy must reflect the big picture or the grand conception and cannot rely on emerging or incremental approaches to establishing a strategy.

- *Strategies must be explicit and simple.* Since the strategy needs to be communicated to the entire organization, simplicity is key.

- *Structure or implementation follows strategy.*

The classic symbol of this school is the famous picture of Thomas Watson Sr. of IBM sitting beneath a sign that says THINK. The primary contribution of the Design School is that it provided the foundation for the development of the other schools.

The Planning School—Strategy Formation as a Formal Process

The Planning School emerged in the mid-1960s. It has resulted in a plethora of strategic planning models.[6] The underlying foundation of all of these models is straightforward: divide the SWOT model into neatly delineated steps, complete with checklists and process techniques, and establish objectives at the front end of the process and the elaboration of budgets and operating plans at the back end.

The planning process articulated by this school includes the following steps:

- *Set Objectives:* Establish and, wherever possible, quantify the goals or objectives of the organization.

- *External Audit:* Assess the external environment (usually using a SWOT analysis) and create a set of forecasts about the future. More recently, this process has been called scenario planning; since predicting the future is difficult, speculating about alternative futures or scenarios might suggest new strategies that would have a great impact on the organization.

- *Internal Audit:* Typically this process is assisted by checklists and tables of topics to consider.

- *Strategy Evaluation:* Organizations can use a variety of techniques ranging from return-on-investment (ROI), to risk analysis, to calculating shareholder value.

- *Strategy Implementation:* This step creates a very detailed and formalized action plan. Objectives, strategies, budgets, and programs are all brought together into a "master plan."

One of the problems with the Planning School approach is that control becomes centralized, and after a few years the planning process becomes more important than the organization's ability to deliver competitive products or quality services. Also, there is not much room for flexibility in dealing with a changing environment since plans are designed to promote a clear sense of direction.

Seven Deadly Sins of Strategic Planning[7]

1. Planning staff took over the process.

2. The process was dominated by planning staff.

3. Planning systems rarely produce desirable results.

4. Planning focused more on mergers and acquisitions at the expense of the core business.

5. Planning failed to examine true strategic options.

6. Planning neglected the organizational and cultural requirements of strategy.

7. Centralized forecasting was inappropriate in an era of restructuring and uncertainty.

The biggest problem for the Planning School approach is that no amount of analysis will result in identifying a strategy or set of strategies that will be beneficial for the organization. The process of planning does not lead directly to strategy formation.

The Positioning School—Strategy Formation as an Analytical Process

The Positioning School began in 1980 with the publication of Michael Porter's classic book *Competitive Strategy*.[8] The significance of this school is that it emphasized the importance of strategies themselves. This school suggests that a few key strategies are desirable in any given industry, especially those that can be defended against existing and potential future competitors. Most important, strategies should be unique to a particular organization.

The premises of the Positioning School include the following:

- Strategies are generic, identifiable positions in the marketplace.

- The context (marketplace) is primarily economic and competitive.

- The selection of the generic strategies by a specific organization is based on a process of analysis.

- Although analysts play a role in the process by sharing the results of their analysis, the managers within the organization control the final choices.

- The market structure and the "position" of the organization within the marketplace drive the deliberate positional strategies, which thus shape the structure of the organization.

In 1985 Michael Porter offered a foundation upon which to build various concepts in *Competitive Advantage*.[9] Porter's model identifies five forces in an organization's environment that influence competition (see Figure 3.1):

- *Threat of New Entrants:* Any new player in an industry must overcome certain "barriers to entry." These barriers may include capital requirements and customer loyalty to established brands.

- *Bargaining Power of Suppliers:* The inevitable tension that exists between a customer and a supplier. The more options for a customer, the less strength for the supplier. In some cases, the supplier's power evaporates when the product or service becomes a commodity.

- *Bargaining Power of Customers:* A customer may wish to receive a higher quality product or service or pay at a lower price. The customer is able to do so depending on the total amount of its purchases, its willingness to use other suppliers, and information about the performance of other suppliers.

- *Threat of Substitute Products/Services:* Innovation in one market may affect other markets. For example, consider the impact next-day courier services, fax machines, and e-mail have had on the postal service.

- *Intensity of Rivalry Among Competing Firms:* Firms employ a variety of tactics or strategies as they attempt to gain an advantage in the marketplace.

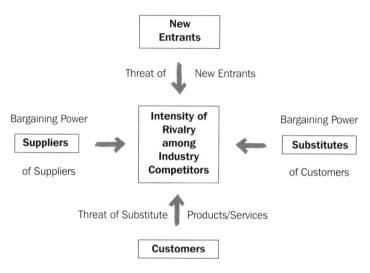

Figure 3.1. Forces That Affect Competition. Adapted from materials by Michael E. Porter, *Competitive Advantage: Creating and Sustaining Superior Performance* (New York: The Free Press, 1985).

Porter also asserted that there are three broad generic strategies:

1. *Cost Leadership:* Organizations that use this strategy are attempting to be the low-cost producer in an industry. Firms might employ economies of scale, leveraging their experience, monitoring quality, and so forth.

2. *Differentiation:* This approach relies on developing unique products or services. With unique offerings and better performance, an organization can justify charging a higher price.

3. *Focus:* This strategy serves specific market segments or niches.

The Positioning School is oriented toward economic and quantifiable measures while ignoring social and political concerns when establishing strategy. Perhaps most important, this school's approach is generic and provides little guidance about how to achieve a unique strategy for a particular organization.

The Entrepreneurial School—Strategy Formation as a Visionary Process

The central thesis of this school, which began in the 1990s, is *vision*. The vision sets a direction and serves as an inspiration that will motivate the employees of an organization. The vision establishes the broad sense of direction while preserving flexibility to adapt to changing conditions.

One of the advocates of the Entrepreneurial School is Peter Drucker, who identifies entrepreneurship with management itself: "Central to business enterprise is . . . the entrepreneurial act, an act of economic risk-taking. And business enterprise is an entrepreneurial institution."[10] Entrepreneurs in large business organizations include Richard Branson of Virgin and Jack Welch of General Electric. Strong leaders share the following approaches to strategy making:

- Strategy making is dominated by the active search for new opportunities.

- Power is centralized in the hands of the chief executive.

- Strategy moves forward by making "large" decisions in the face of uncertainty.

- Growth is the dominant goal.[11]

The premises underlying the Entrepreneurial School include the following:

- Strategy is developed by the organization's leader and provides a vision of the future.

- The leader promotes the vision with a dedicated passion and maintains close control over the implementation to make adjustments as needed.

- Strategy formation is rooted in the experience and intuition of the leader.

- Strategic vision is deliberate in its broad view and flexible in how to achieve the vision.

- The organization is responsive to the leader's directives.

- The strategy often focuses on market segments or niches.

Entrepreneurial strategy often occurs in start-up companies and organizations in trouble and needing a turnaround.

The Cognitive School—Strategy Formation as a Mental Process

The Cognitive School, which was started in the early 1990s, focuses on the mind of the strategist, drawing from the field of cognitive psychology. There is a large body of research that suggests that individuals encounter a variety of problems in making decisions, including a search for supportive evidence, the inability to apply the same criteria in similar situations, failure to change one's view in the light of new information to the contrary, and more recent events having a greater influence than past events.

In addition, individuals have different cognitive styles, as noted in the popular Myers-Briggs instrument.[12] The premises of the Cognitive School include the following:

- Strategy formation is a cognitive process that occurs in the mind of the strategist.
- Strategies emerge as perspectives—concepts, maps, frames, and schemas—that shape how people deal with information from the environment.
- The seen world can be represented as a model or constructed.
- Strategies are difficult to formulate and change once implemented.

The challenge of this school is that while strategies are cognitive and the mind can distort the decision-making process, good and creative strategies have been and are being created.

The Learning School—Strategy Formation as an Emergent Process

Started in the mid-1990s, the Learning School's perspective is that people within an organization learn how to use the organization's abilities to change and adapt in a positive manner in order to respond to a changing environment.[13] In short, this school is less concerned with the actual strategy that was formulated than with what it took to get a strategy implemented.

The premises of the Learning School include the following:

- Many individuals in an organization are involved with learning and strategy formulation.
- Strategy making is a process of learning that occurs over time, and formulation and implementation cannot be separated.

- The learning process is focused on assessing action taken to identify what is successful.

- Leadership focuses on facilitating the process of strategic learning.

- Strategies appear as patterns from the past and become plans for the future.

One of the real contributions of the Learning School is that it has provoked a fundamental discussion about strategy at all levels. The school has raised such questions as:

- Who is the architect of strategy?

- Where in the organization does or should strategy formation take place?

- Is separation of formation and implementation possible?

- How deliberate a process is strategy formation?

The Learning School, through such publications as Peter Senge's book, *The Fifth Discipline*,[14] has contributed to the growing literature pertaining to knowledge management. One of the implications of the learning approach to strategy formation is that it is time consuming and expensive and seems to be favored by large and complex organizations.

The Power School—Strategy Formation as a Process of Negotiation

The word *power* means the exercise of influence beyond economic terms (a synonym for power would be *political*). The influence of power from the external environment will affect any organization, and in many cases politics will infuse an organization.

Thus the focus of the Power School, which began in the late 1980s, is that strategy making is a political process. The games that can be played within an organization are many and varied:

- *Alliance Building:* Negotiation of implicit contracts to build a power base

- *Empire Building:* Creating a larger and stronger department

- *Budgeting:* Playing within clearly defined rules to garner more resources

- *Expertise:* Use of knowledge to build a power base

- *Insurgency:* Resisting authority

- *Counterinsurgency:* Fighting back with political means
- *Lording:* Using formal authority to win
- *Rival camps:* Conflict between departments or individuals
- *Whistle-blowing:* Use of privileged information by an "insider" to effect change
- *Young Turks:* A small group seeking to effect change
- *Line versus Staff:* A game of sibling rivalry.[15]

The premises of the Power School suggest the following:

1. Strategy format is shaped by power and politics.

2. Strategies that arise from the political process take time to emerge and are often in the form of positions and ploys.

3. The political process can be internal and use bargaining, persuasion, and, in some cases, confrontation, with shifting coalitions and interests.

4. The organization can also use the political process to arrange for partnerships and coalitions to build its bargaining power.

The contribution of this school is that it has identified the political process as a reality that must be acknowledged and managed but that is not the sole means for making strategies within an organization.

The Cultural School—Strategy Formation as a Collective Process

Organizational culture can be thought of as a system of shared values, beliefs, and meanings held by staff members that distinguish the organization from other organizations. Dimensions of organizational culture include teamwork, honesty, control, decision-making processes, rewards, and conflict, among other aspects. It includes such topics as a dress code, the respect shown to other staff members and customers, myths and legends, and heroes. In some cases the rules governing the conduct of employees are known as "unwritten ground rules."[16]

The focus of the Cultural School, which began in the early 1990s, includes the following:

- Social interaction involving others within the organization is the key to strategy formation. And the emerging strategy will reflect the beliefs and understanding of those within the organization.

- Individuals acquire the organization's beliefs through a process of acculturation or socialization reinforced by formal training sessions.

- Given the unwritten nature of some beliefs, the origins and basis for these beliefs will be obscure or unknown.

- Strategy making is a deliberate process that reflects the patterns of actions taken by the organization.

- As a result of the culture within an organization, strategic change is likely to move slowly and evolve over time. In some cases, the belief within an organization that it is special means that NIH (not invented here) permeates the culture.

The importance of culture cannot be overstated. One large study found that firms whose culture encouraged participation in the decision-making process by staff, sensible work designs, and reasonable and clear goals achieved financial results twice as high as companies that were rated low in these factors.[17]

It often takes a crisis that is understood and appreciated by everyone within an organization to rescue or turn around an organization that is experiencing life-threatening problems.

The Environmental School—Strategy Formation as a Reactive Process

The Environmental School started in the mid-1990s. It views the forces operating outside the organization as active, while the organization itself merely reacts to these outside forces (often called the environment). The primary contribution of this school is that it attempts to bring the overall view of strategy formation into balance. This school suggests that the outside environment, the leadership, and the organization itself are actually responsible for strategy making.

The premises of this school include the following:

- The outside environmental forces are the central actor in the strategy formation process.

- The organization is required to respond to these forces or lose validity in the marketplace.

- Leadership focuses on reading the environmental forces and ensuring appropriate adaptation by the organization.

Also, while some organizations are faced with strategy formation constraints, other organizations, when confronted with the same circumstances, are able to remain flexible and adapt successfully.

The Configuration School—Strategy Formation as a Process of Transformation

The Configuration School, which began in the mid-1990s, attempts to integrate strategy by showing how different dimensions of an organization band together under particular conditions to define "states, models, or ideal types."

The premises of the Configuration School include the following:

- Most organizations can be described as stable—adopting a particular structure that arises from a particular set of strategies.

- Periods of stability are interrupted by periods of significant change or transformation.

- These periods of stability and transformation can best be understood as life cycles of the organization.

- The key to strategic management is to recognize the need for transformation and manage the process of change without having a negative impact on the organization.

- Different schools of strategy formation can be employed at different times; the key is to choose the right school's process depending on the circumstances.

It is important to realize that one or more of the schools can be a useful perspective, depending upon the circumstances within and stage of evolution of a particular organization. Although a specific process for developing strategies within a library will be suggested in later chapters, it is critical to the overall success of strategic planning and management that the most appropriate process be used depending upon the circumstances within the library.

Notes

1. Quoted in Arthur A. Thompson Jr. and A. J. Strickland III. *Crafting and Executing Strategy: Text and Readings*. New York: McGraw-Hill, 2001, 149.

2. Henry Mintzberg, Brusce Ahlstrand, and Joseph Lampel. *Strategic Safari: A Guided Tour Through the Wilds of Strategic Management*. New York: The Free Press, 1998.

3. Philip Selznick. *Leadership in Administration: A Sociological Interpretation.* Evanston, IL: Row, Peterson, 1957; Alfred D. Chandler Jr. *Strategy and Structure: Chapters in the History of the Industrial Enterprise.* Cambridge, MA: MIT Press, 1962; E. P. Learned, C. R. Christensen, K. R. Andrews, and W. D. Guth. *Business Policy: Text and Cases.* Homewood, IL: Irwin, 1965.

4. Richard P. Rumelt. The Evaluation of Business Strategy, in H. Mintzberg and J. B. Quinn, *The Strategy Process.* 3d ed. Englewood Cliffs, NJ: Prentice Hall, 1997.

5. Mintzberg, Ahlstrand, and Lampel, *Strategic Safari.*

6. H. Igor Ansoff. *Corporate Strategy.* New York: McGraw-Hill, 1965.

7. Adapted from I. Wilson. Strategic Planning Isn't Dead—It Changed. *Long Range Planning,* 27 (4), August 1994, 12–24.

8. Michael E. Porter. *Competitive Strategy: Techniques for Analyzing Industries and Competitors.* New York: The Free Press, 1980. See also Michael E. Porter. What Is Strategy? *Harvard Business Review,* November–December 1996, 61–78.

9. Michael E. Porter. *Competitive Advantage: Creating and Sustaining Superior Performance.* New York: The Free Press, 1985.

10. Peter F. Drucker. Entrepreneurship in Business Enterprise. *Journal of Business Policy,* 1 (1), 1970, 3–12.

11. Henry Mintzberg. Strategy-Making in Three Modes. *California Management Review,* 24 (9), 1978, 44–53.

12. Naomi L. Quenk. *Essentials of Myers-Briggs Type Indicator® Assessment (Essentials of Psychological Assessment).* New York: Wiley, 1999.

13. J. Brian Quinn. *Strategies for Change: Logical Incrementalism.* Homewood, IL: Irwin, 1980. See also Charles E. Lindblom. The Science of Muddling Through. *Public Administration Review,* 19 (2), 1959, 79–88.

14. Peter Senge. *The Fifth Discipline: The Art and Practice of the Learning Organization.* New York: Doubleday, 1990.

15. Henry Mintzber. *Mintzberg on Management: Inside Our Strange World of Organizations.* New York: The Free Press, 1989.

16. Steve Simpson and Ron Cacioppe. Unwritten Ground Rules: Transforming Organization Culture to Achieve Key Business Objectives and Outstanding Customer Service. *Leadership & Organizational Development Journal,* 22 (8), 2001, 394–401.

17. D. Denison. The Climate, Culture and Effectiveness of Work Organizations: A Study of Organizational Behavior and Financial Performance. Ph.D. dissertation. Ann Arbor: University of Michigan, 1982. See also John P. Kotter and J. L. Heskett. *Corporate Culture and Performance.* New York: The Free Press, 1992.

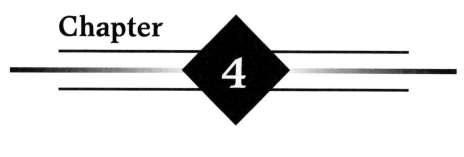
Types of Strategies

> *In a world that is forever changing, the only certainty is change. Therefore, strategies for building the 21st century libraries and librarians must focus on the ability of librarians and libraries to not just adapt to change, but to prepare for it, facilitate it, and shape it.*—Roy Tennant[1]

There are three types of broad or generic strategies that can be considered should any library wish to be more responsive to those it serves: operational excellence, innovative services, and customer intimacy.[2] These broad avenues are interconnected, as shown in Figure 4.1. Excelling in one of these value disciplines means that the organization can significantly differentiate itself from its competitors.

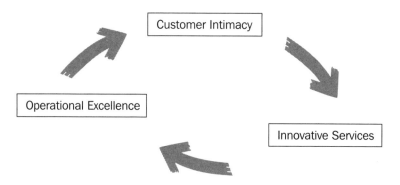

Figure 4.1. Broad Strategies

Operational Excellence

Operational excellence is focused on providing customers with quality services and products delivered with few inconveniences and minimal difficulty. The management literature is replete with articles and books that discuss efficiency-related topics such as activity-based costing, activity value analysis, benchmarking, cost-benefit analysis, and economies of scale.

The customer of the library actually makes a conscious decision to visit the library (in person or electronically), compared to using a competitor, for example, using Google on the Internet, visiting a bookstore (bricks or clicks—Amazon.com), or sending an e-mail to a colleague. Well-known examples of companies that have focused on operational excellence include Dell Computers, Wal-Mart, and Federal Express. These organizations are always seeking ways to improve the speed and quality of service, minimize overhead costs, reduce transaction costs (inconveniences), and reduce departmental boundaries.

When considering operational excellence, questions that a library should address include the following:

- What level of quality can be achieved and maintained for each library service?

- How can technology increase the efficient operation of the library?

- What changes in procedures and processes will lead to improved productivity? The amount of change can be small, using, for example, systems analysis techniques to understand each task and the delays between tasks to accomplish a particular activity, or a radical restructuring known as "process reengineering."[3]

- What barriers to service that presently exist can be eliminated or streamlined? Asking a group of library customers in a focus group about what frustrates them when using the library can be very revealing!

- What economies of scale exist that can be leveraged?

- What performance measures should be used for each service? Has the library benchmarked its services with other libraries known to provide excellent service? Has the library benchmarked with nonlibrary organizations?

The challenge facing any organization that focuses on operational excellence is to ensure that the improvements being made will have a noticeable impact on the customers being served.

Innovative Services

Innovation-focused topics frequently encountered in the management literature include adaptive enterprise, brainstorming, chaos/complexity, creative destruction, double-loop learning, empowerment, entrepreneurship, and so forth. When considering service innovation, a library might ask:

- If there were no constraints, what could we do?
- How can we take our existing service to a new level?
- What service can we discontinue in order to reallocate resources?
- What has never been tried before?
- What are the options, new alternatives, and potential synergies that should be considered?
- Would upgrading our technology base provide the library with the potential for introducing new services or improving existing services?
- Does the library have the talent and skills among existing staff to meet the challenge of innovation?

In the private sector, for example, Mobil NA Marketing and Refining introduced its "SpeedPass"™ system and quickly moved into a dominant position in the marketplace. Mobil "discovered" this innovation when a customer who was participating in a focus group indicated that what he wanted was something he could wave at a gas pump and then immediately start pumping gasoline. Mobil relied on radio frequency identification or RFID technology to uniquely identify each SpeedPass customer. Perhaps the library might consider using RFID technology for introducing a new service or reducing the frustrations associated with an existing service.

Customer Intimacy

Customer intimacy means segmenting and targeting markets with tailored offerings to match the needs of that particular niche. A number of organizations use additional information about customers, freely provided by the customer, to tailor their service offerings to make them more responsive to the needs of each customer. Customer intimacy approaches that work effectively include providing optional personalization services such as that found on Amazon.com (book recommendations based on what other people bought and, by implication, book recommendations based on what the customer has previously borrowed from the library), providing different services and different levels of service to various segments of the marketplace, and so forth.

The management literature has discussed at some length the importance of becoming close to the customer by addressing such topics as attention management, brand management, business modeling, core competence, corporate culture, and customer relationship management.

There is a fair amount of literature showing that customer orientation is positively correlated with organizational performance.[4] Focusing on customer intimacy means that several questions should be addressed:

- What is the library's competitive advantage?
- Who is the competition?
- How can we better serve our existing customers?
- What new segments of all the potential customers can be targeted?
- What share of the market can we expect given our resources?
- Do we know what different types of customers really want and value?

Having a greater understanding of the needs of the library's customers and how the library adds value will allow the library to develop new services or significantly improve an existing service. As these services are incorporated into routine library service offerings, they will be more highly appreciated and valued by the customers of the library. Organizations that focus on service leadership do so by recognizing and embracing ideas from outside the organization and then quickly transforming those ideas into a service offering.

> *Neither results nor resources exist inside the business. Both exist outside. The customer is the business.*
>
> —Peter Drucker[5]

Strategic Options

As noted above, the three broad strategies that a library may follow include operational excellence, customer intimacy, and innovative service leadership. Specific strategies that an organization, including the library, can choose to adopt in pursuing these broader strategies, are discussed below.

Focus

Many libraries attempt to be all things to all people. Yet there is compelling evidence suggesting that such a strategy is destined to result in mediocre service for most customers. Alternatively, the library might focus on providing one or two superior service offerings at selected locations. In some cases, the literature refers to this strategy as differentiation. Typically an organization can focus using one of three approaches:

- *Product/Service Focus:* Most libraries, especially larger libraries, offer a plethora of services that have evolved over time. The problem with this approach is that none of the services provided is performed in an excellent manner. The alternative is to choose two or three services and to focus on doing them well. Depending on the services selected, the library should understand that users and library staff have different roles to play, that different resources, supporting technologies, mix of staff skills, and physical space will be needed. The goal is to develop the library's reputation as "the" source for quality information and services.

- *Geographic Focus:* Another option is to focus on providing library services to specific areas of the community or organization being served. Libraries have long followed this approach as they build and maintain branch libraries.

- *Market Segments:* Another approach is to identify specific segments of the population being served and focus the library's services on a specific group or groups. This approach is often referred to as segmentation. Niche strategies involve concentrating on specific (usually limited or narrow in scope) segments and developing a service that is appealing to this group.

> *The greatest mistake managers make when evaluating their resources is failing to assess them relative to their competitors.*
> —David J. Collins and Cynthia A. Montgomery[6]

Differentiation

As noted in the following list, there are a number of ways in which the library can differentiate itself from its competitors.

- *Quality:* The library can provide access to information resources that have been vetted as to their accuracy, timeliness, thoroughness, and so forth. The library's customers know they will save time when searching for information since the available resources will be of high quality. Too often, the realities of Mooers's Law—"An information retrieval system [library] will tend not to be used whenever it is more painful and troublesome for a customer to have information than for him not to have it—are ignored."[7]

- *Customer Orientation:* The use of the word "customer" rather than *patron* or *user* suggests that individuals have a choice and can "vote" both with their feet (not returning to the library) and, in some cases, their pocketbooks (not voting in favor of a library tax increase or bond issue, or not authorizing an increase in the library's operating budget) should their perception of the service they receive not meet their expectations. The library might embrace a strategy that attempts to provide a more personalized set of services, including:

  - *Standardized Personalization:* The customer might choose from a set of optional predefined services.

  - *Tailored Personalization:* An existing service is modified to meet the needs on demand.

  - *Customized Personalization:* A specific product or service is provided to a limited number of customers. Such services are very labor-intensive and often result in high-quality custom reports, for example.

  The library might begin to collect customer preference information (for example, reading interests, automatic placement of a hold when a new book is published by a particular author, and so forth) as a means to provide some of these personalized services.

- *Innovation:* Given the plethora of information resources and the competition that libraries now face, perhaps its time to consider ways in which the library can innovate and provide clear value to its customers. In private industry, some government agencies, and non-profit organizations, innovation is the key to the continued success of the organization.

- *Technical Superiority:* Perhaps the "key" technical superiority that librarians bring to the table is that they are trained on how to provide access to a diverse body of information resources. The key organizing tool that libraries employ to accomplish this task is to create, maintain, and enhance the library's catalog so that it provides access to high-quality information resources—regardless of their location. Yet the mere fact that libraries have always provided the catalog means that its contribution is rarely understood or acknowledged. Perhaps this "strength" should be more aggressively marketed by the library to demonstrate one of its value-added activities.

- *Distribution:* Libraries located in larger organizations and communities typically build and maintain branch libraries so that their customers are better served. Information resources are routinely moved from location to location to meet a request from the library's customer. And some libraries are extending their distribution by providing access to the library's collection and 24/7 online reference services using the Internet.

- *Support:* Some libraries have provided additional value by providing a variety of help desks, including assistance with information technology problems, student homework assistance, delivery of text and graphics on-demand of rare materials, and so forth.

- *Installed Customer Base:* The library has a very important asset: information about its customers (name, mailing address, e-mail address, and so forth). This information is rarely used by the library to inform its customers of new services, new materials that might be of interest to the customer, and so forth.

- *Name:* The library has an associated brand name or image that carries with it a certain set of both positive and negative stereotypes or expectations. Surprisingly, most libraries do little to enhance the positive aspects of the library "brand." In some cases, the library has decided to not use the word "library" due to historical stereotypes and thus may call itself an "information center" or other nonlibrary name.

  The public library district in London's East End decided to close seven branch libraries and replace them with seven radically new "Idea Stores" to eliminate the perception of the library as a quaint, outdated, and obsolete institution. The libraries are using retail-style branding and image promotion to more aggressively market the "concept" of the library.[8]

- *Change service offerings in existing markets:* A change in a service offering can be effected in several ways, including the following:

  - *Expand service offerings:* The library might introduce a new service to a group previously not served.

  - *Narrow or refocus service offerings:* The library might stop providing a service that is infrequently used or is expensive to maintain when compared to the costs of providing other services.

  - *Improve quality of service:* The quality of service could be improved by the time it takes to complete a task, the accuracy of the service, the timeliness of the service, the completeness, and so forth.

Service/Product Usage

The library could effect an increase in the usage of a service or product by doing one or more of the following:

- *Increase the frequency of usage:* The library might be able to increase the frequency of use of its collection or a service by increasing the value the library customer receives, for example, by relaxing restrictive circulation policies, eliminating barriers to use, and so forth.

- *Increase the quantity used:* Library customers might borrow more items each time they visit the library if they are somehow informed of available resources they might find of value.

- *Find new applications for current users:* Library customers who currently use the library infrequently might be encouraged to use library services more frequently.

- *Improve service utility:* The library has a wealth of information about its collection that is never shared but would be of value to the customer. For example, the library could display the results of a subject search by listing the most heavily used materials first (using circulation data). The library might allow its customers to post comments and reviews about a title, or provide an automatic referring service that indicates that if customers are interested in a particular book, then they might also be interested in these other five to seven titles (based on what other customers have borrowed from the library).

Synergy

The library might explore ways in which its customers can add value so that other library users will benefit:

- *Enhance customer value:* The library might allow library users to add comments, write a review, and rate an item in the library's collection, similar to what can be done when visiting Amazon.com. The library might license access to various complimentary databases that provide book reviews, images of book covers, summaries, biographical information about authors, and so forth.

- *Reduce operating costs:* The library might wish to explore options that reduce the operational costs for providing a service so that the freed-up funds can be used for another purpose.

As shown in Table 4.1, the majority of strategies that might be of value for a specific library are focused on "customer intimacy."

Table 4.1. Strategic Value Disciplines

Strategic Option	Operational Excellence	Customer Intimacy	Innovation
Do nothing			
Focus			
Product/service focus	X	X	X
Geographic focus		X	
Market segments		X	
Differentiation			
Quality	X		
Customer orientation		X	
Innovation			X
Technical superiority	X		
Distribution		X	
Name		X	
Customer base		X	
Service Offerings			
Expand service offerings		X	
Narrow service offerings		X	
Improve quality	X		
Increase Usage			
Frequency of use		X	
Quantity used		X	
Improve service utility		X	
New applications		X	
Synergy			
Enhance customer value		X	
Reduce operating costs	X		

To create superior value, two types of knowledge are required: having a clear understanding of what customers value, and organizing the library's resources to respond to customer needs. In most libraries, there is a total disconnect between the daily actions of managers and activities of staff members and the library's mission statement and vision for the future. Identifying and deciding to utilize a specific set of strategies will assist the library in communicating to all of its various stakeholders *whom* the library is serving, *what* products and services are offered, and *how* the services will be delivered. Strategy is not about *destination* but about the route the library chooses to take—*how* to reach the desired destination. Most important, an effective strategy will differentiate the library from its competitors.

Ultimately, choosing a strategy is about options. As shown in Table 4.2, one of the primary ways of differentiating your library is being better or being different.

Table 4.2. Strategic Choices

Being Better	*Being Different*
Focus on your existing position	Identify new or unexplored customer segments to focus on (a new *who*)
Try to improve your position	Identify new customer needs that no competitor is satisfying (a new *what*)
To make improvements, organizations will focus on quality programs, process reengineering, employee empowerment, and so forth	Identify new ways of delivering and distributing your products and services (a new *how*)

Notes

1. Strategies for Building 21st Century Libraries and Librarians, in *Robots to Knowbots: The Wider Automation Agenda. Proceedings of the Victorian Association for Library Automation 9th Biennial Conference, January 28–30 1998.* Melbourne, Australia: VALA, 1998, 503–7.

2. Michael Treacy and Fred Wiersema. Customer Intimacy and Other Value Disciplines. *Harvard Business Review*, 71 (1), January/February 1993, 84–93.

3. Michael Hammer and James Champy. *Reengineering the Corporation: A Manifesto for Business Revolution.* New York: HarperBusiness, 1993. See also David Osborne and Ted Gaebler. *Reinventing Government: How the Entrepreneurial Spirit Is Transforming the Public Sector.* New York: Addison Wesley, 1992.

4. See, for example, Bernard Jaworski and Ajay K. Kohli. Market Orientation: Antecedents and Consequences. *Journal of Marketing,* 57, July 3, 1993, 53–70; Flora Kokkinaki and Tim Ambler. *Marketing Performance Assessment: An Exploratory Investigation into Current Practice and the Role of Firm Orientation.* Report No. 99-114. Cambridge, MA: Marketing Science Institute, 1999; John C. Narver and Stanley F. Slater. The Effect of a Market Orientation on Business Profitability. *Journal of Marketing,* 54, October 1990, 20–35; Stanley F. Slater and John C. Narver. Does Competitive Environment Moderate the Market Orientation-Performance Relationship? *Journal of Marketing,* 58, January 1994, 46–55.

5. Peter F. Drucker. *Managing for Results.* New York: Harper & Row, 1964, 5.

6. Quoted in Arthur A. Thompson Jr. and A. J. Strickland III. *Crafting and Executing Strategy: Text and Readings.* New York: McGraw-Hill, 2001, 112.

7. C. N. Mooers. Mooers's Law: Or Why Some Retrieval Systems Are Used and Others Are Not. *American Documentation*, 11 (3), 1990, 1.

8. Thomas Patterson. Idea Stores: London's New Libraries. *Library Journal*, 126 (8), May 1, 2001, 48–49.

Part 2

Strategic Planning

What Is Strategic Planning?

Usually, the main problem with life conundrums is that we don't bring to them enough imagination.—Thomas Moore[1]

In its simplest terms, strategic planning is a process to develop an organization's strategic plan. And a strategic plan consists of an organization's mission statement and strategic vision, near-term and long-term performance targets, and the strategies that will be employed to achieve the vision's goals and objectives.

For some, and perhaps most, organizations, including libraries, strategic planning is a periodic formal process that can consume a fair amount of time and effort. For many involved in the process, there seems to be little discernible outcome from the investment other than a planning document that is revised, updated, and then placed back on the shelf. This can be amply demonstrated by the fact that business as usual continues apace after the library has completed its strategic plan!

In general terms, strategic planning should be a continuous and systematic process in which the members of an organization involved in planning make decisions about its future, ensure that procedures and operational policies are designed to achieve the future, and determine how success is to be measured. A few keywords in this definition require further elaboration:

- *Continuous* suggests that strategic planning should be an ongoing process and not a periodic event to produce an update to a planning document.

- *Systematic* underscores the reality that strategic planning is a structured and deliberate process.

- *Process* recognizes that the primary benefit of strategic planning is to think strategically about the future and how to get to it.

- *Members* involved in strategic planning are usually the library's top management team as well as selected other employees.

- *Procedures and operational policies* recognize that a wide range of actions and activities will be required to achieve success. These actions range from specifying long-term goals that are driven by the library's vision to the appropriate allocation of resources.

- *How success is measured* is a key factor in strategic planning so that the library will know that it is making progress toward achieving its goals. The majority of statistics and performance measures historically collected by libraries have little to do with measuring the success of achieving a strategic plan.

Strategic planning can be a significant opportunity to unify management, staff members, stakeholders, and customers through a common understanding of where the library is going, how everyone can work to achieve a common purpose, and how the library will measure and report its progress and levels of success.

Although alternative methods for conducting the strategic planning process are presented in a subsequent chapter, one of the most important perspectives that must be maintained in the planning process is a focus on the customer.

A customer-driven organization maintains a focus on the needs and expectations, both spoken and unspoken, of current and future customers. An exploration of some of these terms will be helpful:

- *Focus:* The library actively seeks to examine the services, products, and processes through the eyes of the customer

- *Needs and Expectations:* Customers' requirements and preferences, as well as their standards for performance, timeliness, and cost, are all part of the planning process

- *Spoken and Unspoken:* Careful listening to the expressed needs and expectations of customers is only one-half of the equation. The "other" half of the planning process is based on information about customers from independent sources.

- *Present and Future:* Customers are the focus for planning and the needs of customers drive the operations of the library.

The planning process must make sure to differentiate between what customers say they want and what they actually do want. Libraries must do more than ask customers what would satisfy their needs, because the customers may not know what their needs actually are.

Once a set of strategies have been created, they should be subjected to a series of challenging questions regarding the scope of the strategy, the choices that underlie the strategy, and the process used to develop the strategies. Potential challenge questions might include the following:[2]

Questions about Scope

- What assumptions about market trends, competitors, new Internet-based entrants, changes in technology, and customer needs have been made? If the assumptions are wrong, will new strategies be necessary? Is use of your library services stable, increasing, or declining?

- Are there trends that could force you to change the way you do business?

- How do you define the market segments that you serve? Want to serve? Are you aware of your market penetration? If yes, is it good, acceptable, or weak?

- Have you considered using new technologies to reach more customers? Provide new services?

Questions about Choices

- What strategic choices are you making, and what are you rejecting? What circumstances or situations would cause you to choose differently?

- Is it possible to change a basic assumption generally held by most libraries? What would be the benefit if the change were made?

- Are you aware of whom your competitors are? What is the value proposition for each competitor? What is your library's value proposition?

- What actions have your competitors taken in the last three to four years that have impacted your library? What could a competitor do that would cause a serious reduction in the number of customers using your library?

- What can the library do that will seriously affect the marketplace and the library's customers?

- Has the library considered outsourcing some activities?

- Does the organizational structure best support the strategies selected by the library?

Questions about Process

- How many customers were interviewed? How many non-customers?

- How did you identify your competitors?

- What approaches were used to develop creative or breakthrough strategies?

- Have you committed sufficient resources to your strategic initiatives?

- What performance measures are used? Is the library achieving its targets? Have the library's processes been benchmarked to determine if they are efficient?

Obviously it is possible to develop additional challenge questions that will assist the library in testing the value and utility of the strategies that have been selected.

Notes

1. *Care of the Soul: A Guide for Cultivating Depth and Sacredness in Everyday Life*. New York: Perennial, 1994.

2. Sarah Kaplan and Eric D. Beinhocker. The Real Value of Strategic Planning. *MIT Sloan Management Review*, 44 (2), Winter 2003, 71–76.

Chapter

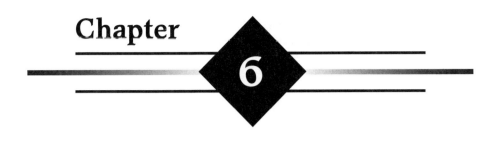

6

Value of Strategic Planning

All our knowledge has its origins in our perceptions.—Leonardo da Vinci[1]

Why should a library be concerned about strategic planning at all? Clearly such an exercise is going to consume resources and the time of those involved in the planning process. In short, what's in it for the library? Unmistakably there is a range of benefits associated with the strategic planning process. Given the rapid pace of change confronting libraries of all types, a library can gain the most benefits from having a shared view of goals and direction of the library.

More than 25 years ago Richard De Gennaro made an astute observation about the pace of change and the opportunities for a library that is still true today:

> The forces that have been transforming the library during the last decade are intensifying and accelerating. We will have to move quickly and decisively to take advantage of the opportunities such a climate of change offers. The library can either ride the wave this wave of change or be overwhelmed by it. I believe we can and should ride it.[2]

When people speak about planning, more often than not they are referring to long-range planning. As shown in Table 6.1, there are significant differences between long-rang planning and strategic planning. Typically, long-range planning extrapolates from the past, has a relatively short planning time horizon, and only makes incremental changes to what presently exists.

Table 6.1. Long-Range versus Strategic Planning

	Long-Range Planning	*Strategic Planning*
Perspective	Narrow focus	"Big picture"
Time Frame	Short—one to three years	Long—five years or more
Thinking	Quantitative analysis	Qualitative synthesis
Orientation	Bottom up	Top down
Forecasts	Rose colored or optimistic	Explores options
Improvements	Incremental	Risk taking
Planning Process	Structured	Explores options
Change	Little change	Considers eliminating services
Orientation	Inward	Customer-focused
Decision Making	Based on subjective evaluations	Based on objective performance measures
Problem Solving	Reactive	Proactive
Management Time	Current operational issues	Broader strategic issues
Focus or Sense of Direction	Fuzzy	Clear to all
Risks	Few—more of the same	More—willing to consider significant change
Goal Setting	Based on operational needs	Based on the library's mission and vision
Results	Making assumptions about the library's performance	Evaluating outcomes using a variety of performance measures

A library that engages in strategic planning is likely to be the beneficiary of several of the following positive outcomes:

- Library services will be more effective and successful in meeting the needs of the library's customers. As a result of meeting with customers, analyzing actual use of the library, and customer satisfaction surveys, and all of the other activities associated with the strategic planning process, the library will more likely provide services of more value to its customers.

- Staff members will have a better understanding of the goals and direction for the library. This will result in their being in a better position to make daily decisions about the focus and priorities of their activities.

- The actual preparation and writing of the plan itself will assist in clarifying the thinking of those involved in the planning process. The resulting planning document will also be useful in communicating with a variety of stakeholders.

- Customers are likely to be more satisfied with the services provided to them by the library, whether the services are provided from within the library or accessed remotely.

- The library is able to allocate resources to achieve the best results.

- Critical issues, constraints, and problems will likely be identified and strategies developed to address them.

- There is a frame of reference for budgeting and addressing short-term operational issues.

- Strategic planning helps the library's management team make resource allocation decisions, since all will know the goals and strategies.

- Staff will have a better understanding of the changing environment and the library's ability to adapt to it.

- Morale and team spirit among all staff members are likely to be higher since they will all know where the library is headed and why. They can assist one another in providing quality library services because there will be a clear understanding of what is expected.

- The library's stakeholders, especially the funding decision makers, will have a better understanding, as the library will be able to communicate its strategic direction.

- The library will not only be able to communicate its goals and objectives to its customers and stakeholders, but it should be able to develop a more effective marketing campaign to communicate the many benefits and the value of using the library.

- The library's core competencies and the importance of its information technology infrastructure will be identified. The need for upgrades to the network, hardware, software, and staff skills will become apparent and can be addressed.

- With a clear focus, the library can explore the possibility of moving to a team-based organization rather than the traditional hierarchical organization. Some libraries have found that teams improve productivity, and individuals have a greater sense of accomplishment and job satisfaction.

- Having a clear purpose, all staff members will better understand the relationships and roles of each individual and how they contribute to serving the library's customers.

- The library will be able to set "Big Hairy Audacious (some will say "Achievable") Goals" and objectives, which will assist in moving the library's services up "another notch."

- Members of the planning committee will have an opportunity to interchange ideas and concepts that will stimulate the creativity of the team. This "team building" process will help members adopt a broader perspective and view problems, opportunities, and structure in a new light.

- When opportunities arise, the library will be better able to assess the potential risks and benefits of new ideas—especially in terms of assessing the value the library provides to its customers. Given a clear sense of direction, the library can be flexible in terms of which tactics it employs to achieve its desired results.

- Having a strategic plan will help the library attract additional resources because the funding decision makers will better understand the value of the library.

- The library can pick up the pace and become energized.

Notes

1. Edward McCurdy. *The Mind of Leonardo da Vinci*. New York: Dodd, Mead, 1928, 67.

2. Richard De Gennaro. Planning Ahead. *Report of the Director of Libraries, University of Pennsylvania, 1981–82*, December 7, 1982, 1–8.

Chapter 7

Strategic Planning Process Options

Uncertainty—in the economy, society, politics—has become so great as to render futile, it not counterproductive, the kind of planning most companies still practice; forecasting based on probabilities.—Peter Drucker[1]

Introduction

One of the most popular planning models is the Plan, Do, Check, and Act cycle, or PDCA, shown in Figure 7.1.

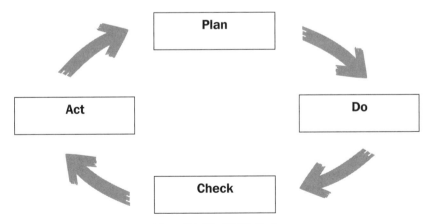

Figure 7.1. The PDCA Cycle

65

The first activity, **Plan**, involves the development of a strategic plan. (See "Strategy Formulation" for a discussion of various alternatives in the development and consideration of alternative strategies.) One of the important characteristics of this first step is to identify what performance measures are going to be used to assess the plan. The second step, **Do**, is all about implementation of the plan. The third step, **Check**, allows the library to check actual results against original and interim targets. The fourth step, **Act**, allows the library to make any necessary adjustments in terms of allocating staff and other resources to ensure that the targets will be met.

A variation of the PDCA model, shown in Figure 7.2, provides additional detail about the entire strategic planning process that are more reflective of the situation found in most libraries.

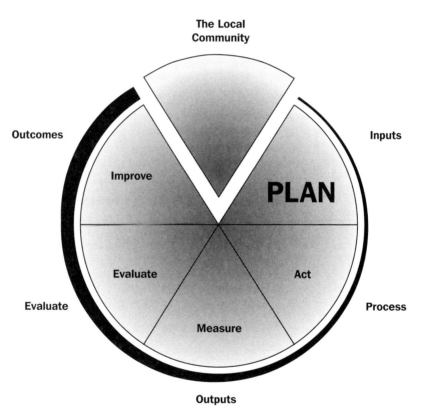

Figure 7.2. The Management-Measurement Cycle

Planning Alternatives

> *If librarians and libraries are to benefit fully from strategic planning, they must first understand and confront the environment in which they work and in which libraries exist.*
>
> —Meredith Butler and Hiram Davis[2]

Fortunately there are a number of alternatives that a library can use to assist in developing a strategic plan, including the following:

SWOT

Scenario planning

Game theory

Decision analysis

System dynamic models

SWOT

> *Why should we look to the past in order to prepare for the future? Because there is nowhere else to look.*
>
> —James Burke[3]

Perhaps the oldest and most popular strategic planning process uses a technique called a SWOT analysis, or an examination of the library's *S*trengths, *W*eaknesses, *O*pportunities, and *T*hreats (see Figure 7.3). An alternative acronym, WOTS UP, is sometimes used (Weaknesses, Opportunities, Threats, and Strengths Underlying Planning). Another label is SOFT: Strengths, Opportunities, Faults, and Threats.

	Internal (within the library)	External (outside the library)
Positive	Strengths	Opportunities
Negative	Weaknesses	Threats

Figure 7.3. SWOT Analysis

In determining the direction and possible strategies of the future of any library, the premise of this alternative is that it is helpful to start by taking stock of current situations, outlooks, and prospects. Assessing the context of the current and likely future environment helps to determine what factors will affect the library. Clearly having good information about the library's competition, knowledge of the library and its parent organization, and knowledge about your marketplace is important. Yet it is not possible to obtain complete and accurate information, and thus the library should focus on developing an awareness of a range of future states.[4]

What trends, government regulations, and technology changes will likely affect the organization? Are the library's competitors known and well understood? How well is your library doing in the competitive environment? (Is use of the library and its services increasing, decreasing, or staying about the same?)

Typically the SWOT analysis starts with an inward or internal focus. The first task is to identify the library's strengths and weaknesses in relation to the marketplace. Each component of the analysis has an impact on the other components as well as the resulting vision for the future, as shown in Figure 7.4.

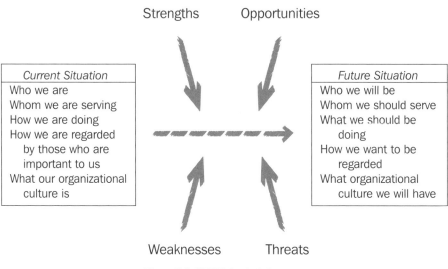

Figure 7.4. SWOT Analysis Impacts

To accomplish this task it is necessary to have a clear understanding of whom the library is and is not serving. A helpful exercise is to complete a market segment and service offering matrix (see Figure 7.5). This will be helpful in identifying any unmet customer needs and will help the library identify market segments that it should focus on and segments it should ignore.

Service Offerings

	Existing	New
New Segments	Unmet needs?	Unmet needs?
Existing Segments	Unmet needs?	Unmet needs?

Figure 7.5. Market Segments and Service Offerings

One of the challenges of preparing a SWOT analysis is achieving a balanced and objective perspective. At times it is difficult to identify the strengths or acknowledge the limitations of the library. The quality of the library's collection, staff, infrastructure, services, programs, and funding, for example, may either be a strength or a weakness. Some libraries have used surveys and focus groups in an attempt to better understand the library and its services from the perspective of the customer. Such surveys are particularly appropriate in the planning process and would be undertaken as a preliminary step in gathering information for use by the team developing the strategic plan.

Once the internal assessment has been completed, attention shifts to an external focus. Here, too, it may be difficult to objectively assess what is happening in the external environment without checking a variety of information resources. One helpful technique is to remember to use the method represented by the mnemonic "TEMPLES" (technology, economy, markets, politics, law, ethics, society) when considering the external arena.[5] Another method sometimes used is the 5Ps (People, Place, Plant, Process, and Product [and Service]). The following questions are involved in the TEMPLES approach:

- *Technology.* What are the important existing and emerging technologies and technology-based standards that might have an impact on the library and its ability to provide new or enhanced services?[6]

- *Economy.* What is happening with the economy, and would a downturn or expansion in the state or local economy have an impact on the library's budget?

- *Markets.* Would the ever-changing marketplace (for information resources and services provided by a library) create a new competitor or provide a new opportunity for the library? For example, are Internet-based reference services (Ask-a-Question services) a threat and/or a resource?

- *Politics*. Is there a change in the political environment that might have an impact on local, state, or national governments?

- *Law*. Are there any federal, state, or local laws that might have an effect on the local library? Changes in administrative law and regulations might also require a change in service offerings at your library.

- *Ethics*. Are there clear policies regarding how the library acquires materials and services? For example, are library policies concerning copyright in compliance with the law and followed by all staff members?

- *Society*. Is society changing in ways that require a reexamination of the mission, goals, and vision of the library? Are the demographic characteristics of the library's customers changing?

An alternative mnemonic, SEPTEMBER, can be used as a checklist to produce a similar analysis. Use of SEPTEMBER ensures that the analysis is more comprehensive and that potential factors are not ignored:

Society

Economics

Politics

Technology

Education

Marketplace

Business

Ethics

Regulations

One of the major hurdles associated with a SWOT analysis is the lack of analysis involved. Often the SWOT analysis is nothing more than a brainstorming session, which identifies specific events and characteristics rather than clearly and carefully asking the planning team to use critical thinking. The end result is a list, often a long list, of things that may have an impact on the library. Consideration must be given to how a specific description is phrased, developing a priority of factors, and ensuring that one statement does not conflict with another. And using a prior SWOT analysis will, in effect, predetermine the results of the current analysis.

Once a prioritized list has been prepared, it should be shared with the team. The team then should assess each statement to determine

- whether the library's customers would agree that the statement clearly represents a strength or weakness, and opportunity or a threat; and

- what specific characteristic or aspect makes a particular factor or statement a strength or weakness, an opportunity or a threat.

The SWOT analysis should include a clearly written description of the results. In some cases, a table is used to present a summary of the analysis, complemented with an elaboration of each factor included in the final analysis. Typically, a summary of these factors is developed to identify the common three to seven themes that emerge as a result of the analysis. These themes are often referred to as "planning assumptions." The assumptions are used as the foundation for the development of strategies that will best met the needs of the library's customers.

Perhaps the greatest shortcoming of a SWOT analysis is that few people are able to look far enough down the road, and thus the analysis typically results in small, incremental changes to existing library plans and strategies.

Scenario Planning

Hindsight is useful for sharpening your foresight.
—Peter Schwartz[7]

An alternative approach to using a SWOT analysis and the development of planning assumptions is to acknowledge that it is difficult to identify a likely single future, and thus developing several alternative visions of the future can be a helpful exercise. Each alternative vision of the future is based on a different set of planning assumptions and is usually referred to as a scenario.

Typically the planning team will identify several scenarios that should be explored. A written description or "story" for each scenario is prepared that identifies the primary planning assumptions used to develop the scenario. For example, a library might consider one scenario as business-as-usual (sometimes called a hybrid library, since the library delivers both on-site and off-site access to electronic and print resources). Another scenario might envision a totally online library delivering services anywhere, anyplace they are needed by the library's customers.

The use of scenarios is helpful because it recognizes that the pace of change is fairly high around the world and that the library's customers do have a choice of whether or not to use the library. The primary benefit of using scenario planning is not to choose a "correct" scenario but rather that multiple futures are considered, which assists in improving decision making about the future of the library and its strategic plans.

Techniques that have been successfully used to develop scenarios include the following:

- *Delphi Studies:* Using an iterative process, drafts of all scenarios are shared with a group of experts. The comments of these experts are incorporated in a subsequent draft that is then shared again with the complete group. Each round of incorporating feedback is continued until there is consensus among all of the experts that each scenario is fairly and accurately described.

- *Trend Extrapolation:* Trends from the past and present are used to forecast the future, with the assistance of statistical techniques.

- *Gaming and Simulation:* In some cases, it is possible to develop a simulation of various factors that will influence the future. One popular simulation game is SimCity™.

Within the business community, the most widely recognized use of scenario planning occurred at Shell Oil in the early 1970s. One scenario they considered was a dramatic rise in the price of oil, which happened in 1973. As the result of their planning process using scenarios, Shell Oil was better prepared to deal with a situation that they had assigned a relatively low probability of occurring.

Developing scenarios requires the use of environmental scanning as well as future visioning to develop a compelling story. Each story starts from a different set of assumptions about the underlying structure and factors that will influence the future. Scenarios are written so that they are engaging and entertaining and usually present both hard data as well as opinions. It is important to remember that the use of scenarios is meant to help people understand and influence the future, rather than to simply react to the scenarios and choose one.

The benefits associated with the use of scenarios will likely include

- providing new understanding of seemingly unrelated factors,

- helping people cope with complexity and uncertainty,

- helping identify cause-and-effect relationships,

- underlining the planning assumptions that have been made to develop each scenario, and

- assisting in understanding the importance of different factors.

Within the library environment, scenario planning has been used effectively in a number of different settings. Consider the following:

- Bruce Shuman developed nine scenarios for public libraries,[8] among which were the status-quo syndrome, everything-to-some scenario, the experience parlor, and the in-the-privacy-of-your-own-home scenario.

- Paul Evans Peters suggested scenarios based on a network-based scholarly communication system targeted to assisting universities and their libraries.[9] The four scenarios are another marketplace for global enterprises, mass customization for and by individuals, knowledge guilds reign supreme, and ivory towers in cyberspace.

- Six scenarios were developed to demonstrate the potential of a networked public library system in the United Kingdom.[10]

Developing effective scenarios takes considerable effort and requires real dedication to achieve high-quality results. Among the actions a library can take to develop useful scenarios are the following:

- Plainly establish the scope of the project in terms of time frame, focus, participants, and the techniques to be used.

- Identify the significant factors, associated uncertainty, and trends that are likely to produce a scenario that is different than the others.

- Develop four or more scenarios (so that a worst case, best case, and middle of the road approach are not allowed to develop).

- Make sure that each scenario is written in a compelling manner, includes both negative and positive features, and has an appropriate and descriptive title.

- Carefully analyze each scenario so that a comparison can be made of the outcomes and impacts.

- Allow time for those involved in the planning process to digest and consider the impacts and ramifications of each scenario.

Game Theory

Game theory is a distinct and interdisciplinary approach to the study of human behavior. The disciplines most involved in game theory are mathematics, economics, and the social and behavioral sciences. John von Neumann, the great mathematician, first put forth the notion of game theory.[11]

Since the work of John von Neumann, "games" have been applied to a much wider range of human interactions in which the outcomes depend on the interactive strategies of two or more persons, who have opposed or at best mixed motives. Among the challenges discussed in game theory are the following:

- What does it mean to choose strategies "rationally" when outcomes depend on the strategies chosen by others and information is incomplete?

- In "games" that allow mutual gain (or mutual loss), is it "rational" to cooperate to realize the mutual gain (or avoid the mutual loss), or is it "rational" to act aggressively in seeking individual gain regardless of mutual gain or loss?

- In what circumstances is aggression rational, and in what circumstances is cooperation rational?

- In particular, do ongoing relationships differ from one-off encounters?

- How does real human behavior correspond to "rational" behavior in these games?

Perhaps the most famous game is called "Prisoners' Dilemma." In this game, two burglars are captured near the scene of a crime and are given the "third degree" separately by the police. Each has to choose whether to confess and implicate the other. If neither man confesses, then both will serve one year on a charge of carrying a concealed weapon. If each confesses and implicates the other, both will go to prison for 10 years. However, if one burglar confesses and implicates the other, and the other burglar does not confess, the one who has collaborated with the police will go free, while the other burglar will go to prison for 20 years on the maximum charge. The two available strategies in this case are: confess or don't confess. The payoffs (penalties, actually) are the sentences served.

The challenge in any game is to determine the consequences of each course of action (decision option) so the strategy tradeoffs can be better understood. Clearly the use of game theory in a library setting would require a significant amount of time and resources to prepare the analysis on which to create and play the "game." Thus, this option for analyzing strategic alternatives in a library setting has not yet been used.

Decision Analysis

Decision analysis makes use of software tools to help users build models that represent specific decision problems, and then relies on statistical analysis to either determine the best course of action or discover what information is required to make a good decision. One of this method's virtues is that it allows decision makers to quantify the uncertainties involved in a decision by expressing them in terms of probabilities. This distinction helps ensure the inclusion of some factors that decision makers might otherwise be tempted to dismiss.

Modeling options include influence diagrams (see Figure 7.6), which show all of the relationships relevant to making a decision, as well as decision trees, which show larger branching structures whose paths represent all of the reasonable alternatives and their outcomes (see Figure 7.7). These models provide complementary approaches to looking at a particular decision problem. Software is available from several suppliers to assist in developing explicit decision-making models.

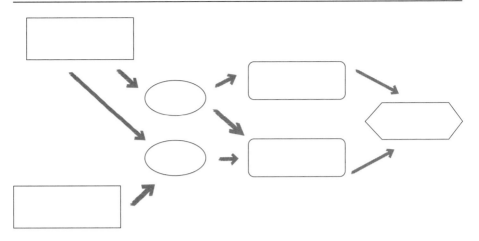

Note: The shape of the node has a meaning.

A decision variable the library can control

An uncertain variable that cannot be controlled

A general variable that is dependent upon other factors

An objective variable that the library would like to maximize or minimize

The arrows denote an influence (does not imply a causal relation).

Figure 7.6. Sample Influence Diagram

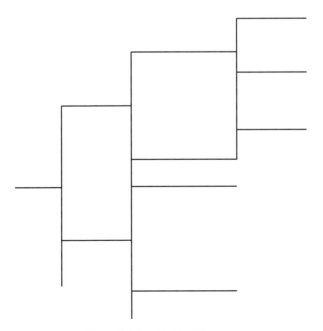

Figure 7.7. Sample Tree Diagram

Decision makers find that mapping alternatives using a decision tree model helps them visualize all of the factors affecting a decision and each of the possible outcomes. Although it might theoretically be possible to test each and every alternative scenario in the real world, few would have the time or resources. By enabling virtual testing, modeling allows decision makers to consider all their possibilities—and provides the timely information needed to take action.

System Dynamic Models

To make sense of reality, we simplify it. These simplifications are called *mental models*. We can simulate our mental models to determine which course of action to implement, which alternative to choose, or which strategies will best achieve our objectives.

History and research show that our choices and decisions are often poor because

- the assumptions constituting the mental models we build are not sufficiently congruent with the reality they are seeking to represent, and

- our simulations of these models do not correctly trace out the dynamic consequences implied by the assumptions in the models.

Systems thinking is an approach that can help us to construct mental models that are more likely to be congruent with reality and to then simulate these models more accurately. By incorporating into the model all of the interactions within a closed system (even simultaneous events that have both short-term and long-term consequences), the system dynamic model allows policy makers to more accurately determine the most effective avenues for producing desired changes over an extended period of time. One of the primary pitfalls with this approach is that a fair amount of the information used to develop the model is based on assumptions or "guesstimates." Thus, the policy makers using such a tool need to be made aware of what data are "good" (sometimes called "hard" data) and what data are "soft" or less reliable.

Software to assist in such models is commercially available, although it must be understood that it would take a fair amount of resources to prepare a strategic planning model for a specific library.

Strategy Formulation

The difference between where the library is now (current status) and where the library wants to be (the vision) is what the library will do (actions), why the library does it (values), and how the library decides to do it (strategies). Thinking about a variety of strategic options opens up the possibility for new alternatives, rather than trying to follow the previously chosen course.

Developing a set of strategies for the library requires persistence, imagination, and a spark of creativity. It really requires that those involved in developing the strategies for the library be able to set aside day-to-day problems and crises to focus on the much more important task of formulating the strategies for the library, creating an implementation plan that acknowledges the challenges associated with the library's culture, and monitoring the progress toward achieving the library's vision.

Once a possible set of strategies has emerged for consideration by the planning team, they can be assessed using a consistent set of criteria. One useful methodology is to use a process called CRITERIA.[12] This methodology has eight elements:

- *Coherence:* Is the strategy consistent with organizational objectives? Will the strategy conflict with existing policies, plans, or procedures?

- *Resources:* Will the required financial, staff, facilities, and information technology infrastructure resources be available when needed? Will capital funding be required? What impact will the strategy have on future budgets?

- *Impact:* Will the strategy result in the library meetings its vision and goals? Will this strategy achieve measurable results?

- *Timing:* Will implementation of this strategy be achieved given existing time constraints? Will any other deadlines have to be adjusted?

- *Environment:* Does the strategy recognize the environmental factors within which the library exists? Possible factors include budgetary concerns, political approvals, infrastructure improvements, and need for staff training.

- *Risks:* How much risk is associated with the implementation of this particular strategy? Will the rewards offset the potential for failure?

- *Insights:* Does the strategy assist the library in delivering value to its customers? Will new suppliers need to be identified and relationships developed?

- *Approval:* Is the strategy clearly understood, and is it acceptable to the various library stakeholders?

Setting Goals and Objectives

Once the library has prepared an analysis of the environment, it then needs to set some goals and objectives. The setting of goals is done with a clear sense of where the library is headed (there is that "vision thing" again). The goals are selected cognizant of the library's overall forte and limitations. Libraries really need to focus on how it is that real value is added by the library in order to improve stakeholders' satisfaction and meet the needs of the customers. Given the goals, it then should be possible to identify strategies that will assist the library in meetings its goals and achieving its vision and eliminate those that will not.

Some libraries have found it to be helpful to use a method developed by Coopers & Lybrand in the 1980s called Priority Based Planning (PBP). The process requires access to budget data and asks managers to identify the minimum level and the associated costs to satisfy essential requirements only. Next, the managers are asked to identify incremental improvements in the service and their associated costs and benefits to satisfy more discretionary levels of service. This information can be particularly valuable when the library is asked to reduce its budget or when additional funding becomes available.

A variation of PBP asks the library's top managers to assign a rating for each service using a 10-point scale:

10   *Essential*—unavoidable requirement
9   *Critical*—real loss or damage to the quality of service
8   *Very attractive*—very important service
7   *Important*—hard to imagine this service being dropped
6   *Significant benefits*—could be dropped
5   *Desirable*—first to be dropped if funding is reduced

<Cutoff point>

4   *Marginal*—first to be supported if funding is increased
3   *Possible*—only if funding increase is substantial
2   *Doubtful*—hard to imagine providing this service
1   *Unlikely*—no service even in the face of a very large budget increase

Again, once the various services offered by the library have been rated, it becomes easier to make decisions about what to do if the budget is increased or reduced significantly.

Critical Success Factors

The starting point is understanding a company's value drivers, the factors that create stakeholder value. Once known, these factors determine which measures contribute to long-term success and so how to translate corporate objectives into measures that guide managers' actions.

—Chris Ittner and David Larcher[13]

One important activity in this phase of the development of strategies is to identify the library's unique capabilities—sometimes called critical success factors or key value drivers. Critical success factors are those things that the organization must be able to do really well to thrive. Among the critical success factors found in a great many organizations are quality, speed, reducing costs, innovation, and customer service. In most industries, there are usually three to six factors that determine success. These factors then become the focus for performance measurement and require the attention of management.[14]

One successful method for developing a library's critical success factors is to have a group of knowledgeable people brainstorm and develop a list of 40 to 50 factors and then combine these into a shorter list. Once the library has identified these factors, they can be compared against the library's processes to determine which factors have the greatest impact on the library's ability to deliver products and services that are valued by the customer.

In a library setting, a group of library and information unit professionals identified the following top 10 critical success factors:

- Competence and qualifications of staff
- Availability and accessibility of staff
- Image of the library and its staff within the organization
- Top management support
- A clear role and purpose of the library
- Quality of information services and products (reliability, currency, etc.)
- Quality of staff assistance and support to users
- Timely delivery of products and services
- People and service orientation of staff
- Responsiveness of staff to user requests.[15]

By implication, the library should also identify those activities that it does not do so well. Activities in this latter category might then become candidates for outsourcing.

The Plan

Although the planning process will provide the most value to those involved, it is important to document the result in a written document. The criticism that most strategic planning documents are out-of-date and thus of limited value is based on the premise that the document itself is static. However, the document can be used as part of a program to communicate the library's plans and strategies to all interested stakeholders.

Preparing a written plan will force those involved to think carefully about the messages being communicated. In most cases, the document will go through several versions as it is edited and polished to ensure that the plan accurately conveys the intentions of those involved in the planning process.

The written document then forms the foundation upon which other materials, such as a PowerPoint presentation, are prepared to communicate the strategies of staff and other interested stakeholders. The plan can also be used as the standard to gauge the progress that is being made as various initiatives and programs are implemented.

In some cases, once the strategic plan has been adopted, some organizations will then prepare shorter versions of the plan in which specific goals and targets are identified. These versions of the strategic plan with a shorter time horizon are sometimes called action plans or business plans.

> **Tip!** One of the best library strategic plans was recently developed by the University of British Columbia Library. Any library—even a nonacademic library—would benefit by examining "Furthering Learning and Research 2004-2007." This plan can be downloaded at http://www.library.ubc.ca/home/planning/.

Caveat Emptor

Given their significant consequences, strategic decisions are generally made with considerable care and deliberation. But after gathering all the available information and completing an often lengthy decision process that may involve costly studies and multiple meetings, many decision makers nevertheless base their final choices on something less than science: gut feeling or their initial impressions.

Executives have a tendency to make decisions based on "delusional optimism" rather than on a rational weighing of gains, losses, and probabilities.[16] Research confirms that instead of trying to come to terms with complexity, decision makers have a marked tendency to push it aside or ignore it. One recent study found that corporate executives now rely more on instinct than on facts and figures in running their businesses.[17] Yet researchers agree that the more complex and difficult a decision, the less likely it is that intuition—when detached from rigorous analysis—will yield positive results.

Notes

1. Planning for Uncertainty. *The Wall Street Journal*, July 22, 1992, A12.

2. Strategic Planning as a Catalyst for Change in the 1990s. *College & Research Libraries*, 53 (5), September 1992, 393–403.

3. James Burke. *Connections*. Boston: Little, Brown, 1978, 124.

4. Tim Hayward and Judith Preston. Chaos Theory, Economics and Information: The Implications for Strategic Decision-Making. *Journal of Information Science*, 25 (3), 1999, 173–82.

5. Simon Wootton and Terry Horne. *Strategic Thinking: A Step-by-Step Approach to Strategy*. Dover, NH: Kogan Page, 2000.

6. See, for example, Joseph R. Matthews. *Technology Planning: Preparing and Updating a Library Technology Plan*. Westport, CT: Libraries Unlimited, 2004, for suggestions on how to develop a technology monitoring program and ways to identify important technology trends.

7. Peter Schwartz. *The Art of the Long View*. New York: Doubleday, 1991.

8. Bruce A. Shuman. *The Library of the Future: Alternative Scenarios for the Information Professional*. Englewood, CO: Libraries Unlimited, 1989. See also Bruce A. Shuman. The Public Library: Some Alternative Futures. *Public Library Quarterly*, 11 (4), 1991, 13–23.

9. Paul Evans Peters. From Serial Publications to Document Delivery to Knowledge Management: Our Fascinating Journey, Just Begun. *Serials Librarian*, 28 (1/2), 1996, 37–55.

10. Library and Information Commission. *New Library: The People's Network*. London: The Commission, 1997. Available at: www.ukoln.ac.uk/services/lic/newlibrary (accessed February 25, 2005).

11. John von Neumann and Oskar Morgenstern. *The Theory of Games and Economic Behavior*. New York: Wiley, 1953.

12. Sheila Corrall. *Strategic Management of Information Service: A Planning Handbook*. London: Aslib/IMI, 2000.

13. *Financial Times* "Mastering Management" supplement, October 16, 2000, 4.

14. John F. Rockart. Chief Executives Define Their Own Data Needs. *Harvard Business Review*, 39 (5), 1979, 111–21.

15. M. Broadbent and H. Lofgren. *Priorities, Performance and Benefits: An Exploratory Study of Library and Information Units*. Melbourne, Australia: Centre for International Research on Communication and Information Technologies & Australian Council on Libraries and Information Service, 1991.

16. Dan Lovallo and Daniel Kahneman. Delusions of Success: How Optimism Undermines Executives' Decisions. *Harvard Business Review*, 81 (7), July 2003, 56–63.

17. Eric Bonabeau. Don't Trust Your Gut. *Harvard Business Review*, 81 (5), May 2003, 116–23.

Chapter

8

Implementation

Strategies are intellectually simple; their execution is not.—Lawrence A. Bossidy[1]

The second step of the planning model, as shown in Figure 8.1, is the implementation activities.

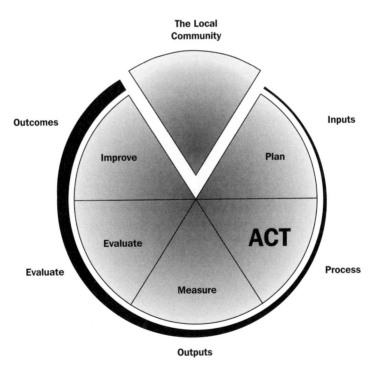

The Local Community

Outcomes

Inputs

Improve

Plan

Evaluate

ACT

Evaluate

Process

Measure

Outputs

Figure 8.1. The Management-Measurement Cycle

There is widespread evidence that once the strategies have been decided upon by any organization, the execution of the particular strategy is more important than the formulation of the strategy itself. Successfully executing the strategy requires a different set of skills than exploring, considering, deciding, and drafting a strategy, as well as the focus of all staff members within the library. In all likelihood, a majority of for-profit and nonprofit organizations fail when attempting to execute their strategy. One study found that 70 percent of chief executive officer failures came as the result of poor implementation rather than the choice of the strategy itself.[2] The obvious question then arises: Why is execution or implementation of strategy so difficult? As shown in Figure 8.2, a number of barriers arise when implementing strategy.

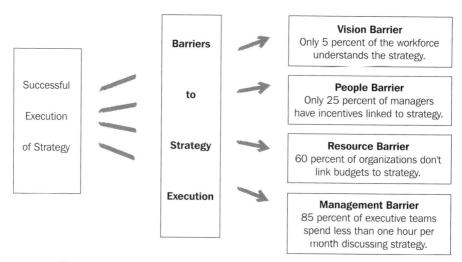

Figure 8.2. Barriers to Implementing Strategy. Adapted from material developed by Robert S. Kaplan and David P. Norton.

The barriers to successfully implementing the desired strategy for a library are many and require concerted action to ensure that they are acknowledged and successfully breached:

- *The Vision Barrier:* Most organizations, including libraries, have a difficult time of communicating the organization's vision and strategies to employees. In part, the hierarchical organizational structure and climate mean that the top management team assumes that the appropriate message gets passed on to all staff members. But making assumptions is dangerous; they are most often proven false.

- *The People Barrier:* Helping people focus on the library's vision and strategies means that the day-to-day problems and situations that need attending to do not mask the longer-term horizon of strategies.

- *The Resource Barrier:* A majority of organizations, and that includes libraries, do not link budgets to strategies; rather the budget process, despite the often lengthy and painful process of preparation, is simply a matter of modifying last year's budget to meet the forecast or fiscal constraints. In reality, the preparation of the budget can afford the library an opportunity to carefully examine priorities for the coming year and link these priorities to the strategic goals and objectives.

- *The Management Barrier:* Most regularly scheduled management meetings typically focus on two topics: responding to problems (putting out the fires) and making sure that the library is staying within its budget. Little time is spent on viewing the library from a broader perspective and ensuring that the day-to-day activities are aligned with meeting the library's vision and successfully implementing the planned strategies.

Another survey found similar problems when it came to discovering the reasons for strategic implementation failures (see Figure 8.3).[3] Strategic control is concerned with answering two questions: Is the strategy being implemented as planned, and are the results what were intended? Clearly areas for improvement include improving the communication of the selected strategies, ensuring that the performance measures reflect the selected strategies, and aligning (changing or modifying) processes to support the strategic implementation.

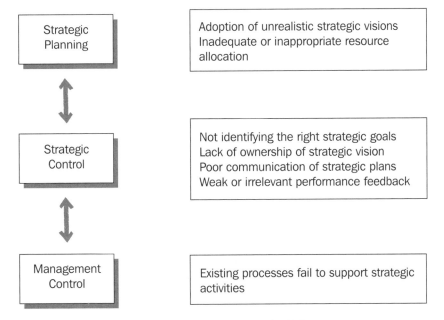

Figure 8.3. Strategic Implementation Failures

> *Managers can't assume that strategy and capa-bility will come together automatically.*
> —Thomas M. Hout and John C. Carter[4]

Starting the Planning Process

Normally a strategic planning memo or statement is issued at the start of the process that informs everyone of

- the purpose and worth of strategic planning,
- who will be involved in the planning process,
- the steps or activities that will be followed in the process, and
- the format and timing of reports.

Such a statement has significant benefits. First, it identifies the sponsorship and support of the planning process. Such legitimacy ensures that the results of the process will be seen as objective and thus reduce anxiety within the organization. Such authorization also helps ensure that those involved in the planning process have access to all necessary documents and information.

Second, the statement also must make clear the link between the strategic plan and other decision-making activities, especially the budget. Third, the statement should ensure that there is a procedure for resolving any disagreements that may arise between the planning committee (or whatever name is chosen for the planning group) and other key individuals and departments within the library.

Fourth, and perhaps most important, the statement must clearly articulate the individual or group that is the champion of the process. In almost all cases, this is the library director, the library board, or a designated member of the top management team.

Who Should Be Involved

In most cases, it is advisable to involve staff from three levels within the library: the top policy decision makers, middle management, and selected staff from the front lines (technical services, automated information services, and public services). Depending on the type of library, it may be prudent to involve in the strategic planning process a member of the library board, city council, board of supervisors, dean or provost, or a manager who controls the library's purse strings.

The participation of the top policy makers is key because they often perceive a mismatch between how the library is doing and the external environment. They are also boundary spanners and are able to link people and other resources that may be needed during the planning process. Mid-level managers should be involved since they are involved in translating policy into operating procedures and activities.

Lower level staff should be involved due to their technical expertise in a specific area or the fact that they will have to live with the results of the planning process on a day-by-day and minute-by-minute basis, and their perspective is important. In short, strategic planning processes should create opportunities for staff at all levels to inform themselves about the library and its environment. The process can empower staff to work creatively and cooperatively as they select appropriate strategies and reach agreement about goals.

In most cases, if the planning group exceeds eight to ten people, then the dynamics of the group change and the process can take longer.

Once a draft of the plan has been prepared, it is crucial for the draft to be shared with key stakeholders to determine their reactions to and enthusiasm for the plan. Among the more likely stakeholders to share the draft with are selected customers, funding decision makers, previous board members, community leaders, and other library directors. Some academic and public libraries have involved several hundred customers by listening to their concerns and comments as drafts of the strategic plan were prepared, in order to be more responsive to their needs.

Strategic Planning Process Tips

- The library director must fully support and sponsor the strategic planning process to give it legitimacy.

- A member of the library's top management team must champion the planning process.

- A strategic planning group (be it called a committee, a task force, or whatever) of appropriate size should be formed.

- The strategic planning group and other policy makers, for example, library board members, may need an orientation and training to assist them in being better members of the group.

- A written statement from the library director should outline the goals, objectives, and time lines for the strategic planning group.

> *Leadership is accomplishing something through other people that wouldn't happen if you weren't there. . . . Leadership is being able to mobilize ideas and values that energize other people. . . . Leaders develop a story line that engages other people.*
>
> —Noel Tichy[5]

What Is Required

Initially, the library director, top management team, and library's board or funding decision makers must decide that engaging in the process to prepare a strategic plan will be a fruitful exercise. Those who are appointed to the planning committee will have to be excused from all or a portion of their regular job responsibilities to be active members of the committee.

The planning committee should decide whether to engage the services of an outside consultant to assist them in the preparation of the plan. If a consultant is engaged, the scope of the consultant's responsibilities must be clearly stated for all concerned, and the library must retain control. The consultant might act solely as a facilitator for some portion of the process, act as a facilitator and be responsible for creating a draft of the strategic plan, and so forth.

The planning committee will need access to a variety of existing documents and information about the library, its customers, and how the existing services are utilized. In addition to providing access to the library budget, prior plans, evaluation reports, and surveys, the library might want to prepare a document that summarizes the current scope and scale of existing services, organizational structure, mission statements, and so forth.

In addition, the library director might ask a planning committee member to prepare an analysis of important trends, views, and attitudes of a variety of stakeholders. An analysis of the library's competitors and a survey of the library customers and non-customers might also provide helpful information during the planning process.

The library director should set the time frame in which the strategic plan must be prepared in draft form. Depending on the size of the library and its parent organization, this may be as short as a few months or as long as three years.

The planning principles and values that should guide the preparation of the library's strategic plan include the following:

- *A Focus on the "Big Picture":* The idea is to develop a plan that addresses all major concerns and issues and acknowledge that not all of the detail-oriented issues will be addressed.

- *Meaningful Participation:* All staff members should feel that their concerns and issues will be heard and addressed in a meaningful way.

- *Sharing the Work:* Members of the planning committee should be selected for their skills and ability to make a contribution to the overall plan.

- *Ownership:* The resulting plan will cause all staff members to make a strong commitment to the successful implementation of the selected strategies and the overall plan. In short, the plan must energize the library's staff members.

- *Strategies:* The selected strategies should be responsive to the library's environment and assist the library in achieving its vision of the future.

- *Setting Targets:* Once the strategies have been developed, a set of performance measures must then be selected so that the library can monitor its progress toward achieving its vision. Goals and interim targets must be established for each performance measure.

How

The Planning Committee must establish clear requirements for who is responsible for what activities as the strategic planning process is followed. The committee should be scheduled to meet on a regular basis to ensure steady progress in the development of the plan. It may be necessary to schedule time to work off-site so that regular day-to-day responsibilities do not interrupt important meetings.

An outline of the table of contents for the strategic plan that will be the result of the planning process should be developed and agreed to at the start of the process. This will help in assigning responsibilities to specific individuals so that the planning process taps the strengths of all those involved.

Responsibility for writing the plan must also be specified. Typically, it is best to assign this responsibility to a single individual rather than assigning sections to each committee member. Once a draft of the plan has been produced, it can be shared with key stakeholders to ascertain their reactions and concerns before any large effort is spent in editing and word crafting the final plan.

Force field analysis is a simple but powerful technique for building an understanding of the forces that will drive and resist a proposed change. The force field diagram is derived from the work of social psychologist Kurt Lewin.[6] Lewin suggested that human behavior is caused by forces—beliefs, expectations, cultural norms, and the like—within the "life space" of an individual or society. These forces can be positive, urging us toward a behavior, or negative, propelling us away from a behavior. A force field diagram portrays these positive or "driving forces" and negative or "restraining forces" that affect a central question or problem (see Figure 8.4). A force field diagram can be used to compare any kind of opposites, actions and consequences, different points of view, and so forth.

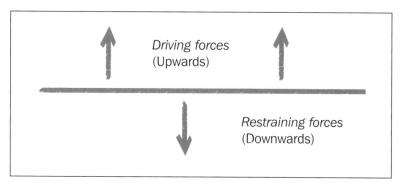

Figure 8.4. Force Field Analysis Diagram

In the context of process improvement, driving forces could be seen as pushing for change, while restraining forces stand in the way of change. A force field diagram is used to analyze these opposing forces and set the stage for making change possible. Change will not occur when either the driving forces and restraining forces are equal, or the restraining forces are stronger than the driving forces. For change to be possible, the driving forces must overcome the restraining forces. Usually, the most effective way to do this it to diminish or remove restraining forces. It can be tempting to try strengthening the driving forces, but this tends to intensify the opposition at the same time.

A force field analysis can be prepared for the strategies being implemented by the library or can be used to assess an existing service. To prepare a force field analysis the following steps should be followed:

- **Step 1.** State the problem or desired state and make sure that all team members understand. You can construct the statement in terms of factors working for and against a desired state or in terms of factors working for and against the status quo or problem state.

- **Step 2.** Brainstorm the positive and negative forces.

- **Step 3.** Review and clarify each force or factor. What is behind each factor? What works to balance the situation?

- **Step 4.** Determine how strong the hindering forces are (high, medium, low) in achieving the desired state or improving the problem state. When the force field is used for problem analysis, the forces with the biggest impact should be tested to determine what causes the impacts. If the force field is used to develop solutions, those factors with the biggest impact may become the focus of plans to reduce resistance to change.

- **Step 5.** Develop an action plan to address the largest hindering forces.

Organizations that have been successful in implementing their strategic plans have acknowledged the following:

- The importance of *communicating* the plan to all stakeholders, especially to all of the library's staff members. Not only do staff members need to know about the strategies, they also need to understand how their jobs will be affected by the new strategies that are being implemented. It is particularly helpful to involve staff in the redefinition of jobs that will be changing as well as offering them the opportunity to attend training sessions to upgrade their skills.

  In addition to understanding the strategies, everyone will have a better sense of the organization's expectations. The performance measures that will be used to assess progress being made in terms of achieving the goals and objectives of the plan will be clearly stated. Objectives that are a stretch but achievable will help move the library to the next levels of providing great service to customers.[7]

- That it may be necessary to provide a range of *training* to the organization's employees so that the skills needed to implement and maintain the strategic course of action will be available. Such training will likely involve the use of outside resources as well as tapping the strengths of selected staff members to share their expertise.

- That problems can and will occur (Murphy's Law never seems to go out of style!). The challenge is how to deal with these problems in a positive manner. Tom Peters and Bob Waterman have suggested "management by walking around" as an effective way for the organization's top and middle level managers to get a better sense of the challenges facing an organization.[8]

Notes

1. Quoted in Arthur A. Thompson Jr. and A. J. Strickland III. *Crafting and Executing Strategy: Text and Readings.* New York: McGraw-Hill, 2001, 229.

2. Ron Charan and Geoffrey Colvin. Why CEOs Fail. *Fortune*, June 21, 1999, 69–78.

3. Ian Cobbold and Gavin Lawrie. *Why Do Only One Third of UK Companies Realize Significant Strategic Success?* Berkshire, UK: 2GC Active Management, 2001.

4. Quoted in Thompson and Strickland, *Crafting and Executing Strategy*, 229.

5. Quoted in Thompson and Strickland, *Crafting and Executing Strategy*, 267.

6. Kurt Lewin. *Field Theory in Social Science.* New York: Harper & Row, 1951.

7. Bill Davidson. *Breakthrough: How Great Companies Set Outrageous Objectives and Achieve Them.* New York: Wiley, 2004.

8. Tom Peters and Robert Waterman. *In Search of Excellence.* New York: HarperBusiness, 1982.

Part 3

Monitoring and Updating Strategies

Chapter 9

A Culture of Assessment

Things are always different—the art is figuring out which differences matter.—Lazlo Birinyi[1]

Measuring more is easy, measuring better is hard.—Charles Handy[2]

The third and fourth elements of the planning model, "Evaluate" and "Update," are shown in Figure 9.1 (p. 96). The evaluation activity illustrates that the library uses several performance measures to determine what progress is being made toward achieving the goals and objectives that have been previously established. The update or revise activities are those corrective actions that are taken to the library's activities and processes so that the goals and objectives will be achieved.

Avoiding some of the more commonly made mistakes will allow the library to move from strategy formulation to implementation with comparative ease. These mistakes include confusing strategies with goals that are derived from the library's vision, not developing the cause-and-effect relationships between strategies and the anticipated goals, failing to identify and implement performance measures that accurately measure the strategy, and not devoting sufficient time and resources to the training and instruction of all employees.[3]

The use of performance measures in almost all libraries has been primarily the result of tradition or a mandate to collect prescribed statistics. Should a library introduce a new measure or measures, they typically are associated with the use of new services such as providing a library Internet Web site or providing access to online databases for direct customer searching.

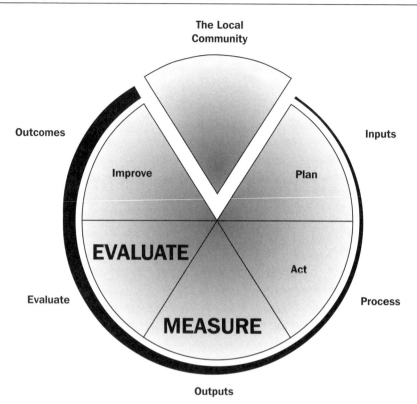

Figure 9.1. The Management-Measurement Cycle.

Rather than relying on tradition, instincts, and a group discussion, a library can embrace a "culture of assessment" in which decisions are based on facts, research, and analysis. The library focuses on planning and delivering services that maximize the anticipated outcomes and impacts for its customers and stakeholders. The library and its staff members have a clear understanding of what customers expect and value. The collection and analysis of data, even data reflecting a small sample size, can be useful in more accurately defining a problem, assisting in revealing activities or processes that may require further study and analysis as well as monitoring the progress that is being made to achieve specific goals and objectives.

The successful application and use of performance measures involves recognizing that this is a political activity, a complex evaluative activity, and an activity that demands appropriate incentives.[4]

> *Strategic management is not a box of tricks or a bundle of techniques. It is analytical thinking and commitment of resources to action.*
>
> —Peter Drucker[5]

It would be optimistic to state that a majority of libraries have developed a "culture of assessment"; sadly that is not the case. A survey of Florida public libraries found that although a wide variety of performance measures were used, the library directors felt that the positive impact of these measures was limited.[6] Few of these libraries relied on customer satisfaction surveys, had concerns about the accuracy of measures, or appreciated the value and utility of employing performance measures. Perhaps, most important, these library directors felt that the performance measures used in their libraries did not reflect the impact of the library on the community that they serve. The data that collected were often isolated, sometimes referred to in the literature as "orphaned data" or "silo data," and not related to a planned program of providing performance measures to either the library management team or interested stakeholders.

This lack of a culture of assessment is most distressing because the use of performance measures in a systematic manner can produce many positive benefits for a library. The collection of data can be the catalyst to move a library in the right direction, make improvements in services to improve productivity and lower costs per transaction, improve customer service, as well as demonstrate the value of the library to its stakeholders.

The data that can be collected by the library include the traditional input- and output-oriented counts and other numeric values used in the majority of performance measures as well as including qualitative data from focus groups, user and staff surveys, and benchmarking activities.

> *The real question isn't how well you're doing today against your own history, but how well you're doing against your competition.*
> —Donald Kress[7]

In particular, libraries must shift their inward-looking focus, which results from the collection and use of input, process, and output measures, to a focus on measures that concentrate on the outcomes or impacts on the individual and the larger organizational context. This outward-looking or customer focus has several implications:[8]

- Customers are the most important part of an organization.

- Attracting new customers and retaining existing customers means you must satisfy their needs.

- The library can't satisfy their needs unless you know what their needs are.

In addition, this customer focus means that staff are likely to abandon the perspective of the traditional, and perhaps limiting, departmental boundaries and identify solutions to problems and opportunities that will be most beneficial to the customer.

A foundation for the use of performance measures in any library requires that the library management team and almost all staff members have a clear understanding of the costs of providing each of the various library services. The use of cost accounting information will enable the library to include all of the cost components for providing a service—staff costs, collection building costs, administrative costs, and other operating costs. With the cost data the library can compare its productivity with comparable libraries and perhaps participate in a benchmarking study.[9]

To achieve the benefits that a "culture of assessment" will bring, Amos Lakos has suggested that:

> [l]ibraries must have an organizational environment in which decisions are based on facts, research and analysis, and where services are planned and delivered in ways that maximize the positive outcomes and impacts for customers and stakeholders. A culture of assessment exists in organizations where staff care to know what results they produce and how those results related to customer expectations. Organization mission, values, structures and systems support behavior that is performance and learning focused.[10]

There are a number of reasons why a culture of assessment and use of performance measures are not frequently found in any library. Among these are the following:

- *Perception That What the Library Does Can't Be Measured:* Clearly it is difficult to assess the impact of the library on its users and its larger organizational setting—be it a community, university, school, government agency, or corporation. But a great many measures have been developed, and with enough creativity and motivation, additional measures can be created that have relevance for a particular library situation.

- *Lack of Leadership:* The library director and to some extent the funding decision makers have no understanding of how the use of performance measures can assist the library in acquiring additional resources and demonstrating the value of the library.

- *Library's Lack of Control over Outcomes:* This exists in most libraries, but it is still possible to demonstrate some measures of outcomes and the impact of the library on the lives of its customers.

- *Unfair Comparisons:* A comparison with other libraries is going to happen—period. By taking the initiative, the library can assist in selecting comparable libraries; you can assist in proactively comparing performance that will be beneficial to your library.

- *Use of Such Information against the Library:* Demonstrating openness and accountability, even when the news is not positive, inspires trust. Being open about what areas need improvement and showing that plans are in place to make enhancements is all that most stakeholders are looking for.

- *Lack of Skills:* The librarians and other staff members feel that they do not have the necessary skills to effectively gather statistics and performance measures through the use of surveys, focus groups, observations, and so forth.

- *Old Mental Models.* Traditionally, librarians have used input and output measures, which are counts of size and activity, as measures of success. There is scant recognition of the need to determine the impact of the library on the lives of its customers through the use of outcome measures.

Amos Lakos asserts that it is possible to change libraries so that they move to embrace a culture of assessment. He suggests that a culture of assessment exists when:[11]

- The library's mission, planning, and policies are focused on supporting the customer's information and communication needs and written documents explicitly acknowledge a customer focus.

- Performance measures are included in library planning documents such as strategic plans. Along with identifying a specific set of measures, a time frame for achieving targets for each measure is defined.

- Library managers are committed to supporting assessment. Use of assessment tools must be encouraged and staff at all levels should be encouraged to participate. Assessment must become a part of the normal work process.

- Continuous communication with customers is maintained through needs assessment, quality outcome, and satisfaction measurements.

- All library programs, services, and products are evaluated for quality and impact. The focus of evaluation must include quality assessments as well as the actual outcomes or impacts of the library on the lives of users. It is important for staff to understand that the assessment will focus on the processes, procedures, and services rather than an evaluation of individuals.

- Staff have the opportunity and resources to improve their skills to better serve users.

> *The choice is clear. Change now and choose our futures. Change later, or not at all, and have no future.*
>
> —Carla J. Stoffle, Robert Renaud, and Jerilyn R. Veldof [12]

Developing a culture of assessment within any library requires the advancement of four initiatives:

Listening to the voice of the customer,

Listening to the voice of the library's staff members,

Listening to the voice of the process, and

Listening to the voice of the organization. [13]

Listening to the Voice of the Customer

Clearly customers for almost any product or service have a plethora of choices available to them today that were not available 10 to 15 years ago. For any organization to prosper, however that is defined, it is critical to develop a better understanding of its customers and how the customers' needs are changing and evolving. New services may be needed, and existing services must be upgraded to take advantage of the potential capabilities of technology. Customers can vote with their feet as well as their wallets in terms of deciding to use a library and the services that it offers or a competing service.

Conducting a customer satisfaction survey on a regular basis is essential for a library; it will learn what is important to its customers and the size of the gap that exists between the customers' expectations and the existing service delivery realities. The development of the LibQUAL+ survey instrument among Association for Research Libraries (ARL) libraries is important; the data are being used to benchmark a library's performance rather than as a rating. [14] The sample size for most libraries using this instrument is quite large, indicating that customers value the opportunity to provide feedback and help shape future improvements.

Another form of customer satisfaction survey that has been used successfully in a library setting is called a priority and performance evaluation (PAPE). [15] For each actual or potential library service, customers are asked to indicate the priority the library should give it using a Likert scale. The customers are then asked to rate the performance in providing the service. After tabulating the results, the library can see what gaps exist between the customers' expectations and the actual services being provided. One library administered the survey to both staff and customers and discovered that staff members tended to underestimate the importance of performing the promised service dependably and accurately.[16]

Regardless of the survey instrument used, the resulting data provide a broad or macro-level view of library services. The information that results from the survey must then be discussed with various groups of customers in focus groups so that the library has a better understanding of why customers responded in the survey as they did. Listening hard and asking customers to share their experiences will do much to help view the library's services from the perspective of the customer. This "listening to the voice of the customer" will ensure that the library understands the perceptions of its customers and the value the library provides rather than drawing conclusions and inferences using the myopic vision of a library's assumptions and beliefs. Employing both macro-view satisfaction surveys as well as micro-view discussions with groups of customers will provide a more balanced view of the "customer experience" when they interact with the library.

Don't wait to be told to learn new skills. Learn them now!

—Anonymous

Listening to the Voice of Library Staff Members

If the focus of the library is on its customers and the quality of the services that they receive, then it is incumbent on the library to foster a culture of customer care. This can be accomplished in several ways:

- The knowledge and experience of staff members should be tapped on an ongoing basis as the library engages in its strategic planning process. The staff members who interact directly with customers are uniquely qualified to reflect the concerns of those customers. Involving staff in the planning process will provide opportunities for them to gain a broader perspective than is normally the case when they provide the same service day after day. And given the accelerating pace of change in most fields, getting staff to volunteer to track the developments in a variety of fields will assist the library in identifying trends that will affect the library.

- Just as forward-looking organizations are focused on continuous improvement, so too must libraries invest in their staff by providing opportunities for continuous learning. This learning can be formalized using specific training sessions or classes as well as taking advantage of on-the-job training opportunities.

Fundamental to the development of a culture of assessment is that staff members must be knowledgeable about and be able to determine what evaluation methodologies, given a range of options, to employ in various situations. In addition, staff members will need to know how to apply the chosen methodology in their particular library setting. A variety of research methodologies exist that can be applied to bettering understanding the processes involved in delivering a service, developing outcome and output measures for a particular service, or selecting various performance measures that will reflect the outcomes of all the library's services.

• Staff must recognize that employing several customer-focused performance measures will assist them in understanding the needs and priorities of customers as well as indicating how they are doing in meeting customer expectations. All types of libraries are being asked to define and account for their performance and demonstrate positive outcomes on the lives of their customers.

Staff need assistance in the form of training to regularly employ the use of performance measures to analyze problems and ascertain their performance. And rather than the traditional internally focused measures, the library should be analyzing the results of externally focused or customer-focused performance measures.

Listening to the Voice of the Process

Knowing your library's products and services do not meet customer expectations is not all that helpful if the library cannot take the next step, to discover the causes of the shortfall.

Library staff members should be encouraged to study and chart existing processes and to use process improvement tools and benchmarking to discover the size of the service delivery gap. While a variety of continuous quality improvement or process improvement techniques can be used in this analysis, a systems approach is often employed. Library staff members should learn how to analyze a system of processes to determine what tasks or activities are performed, what time is required to complete each activity, and how much time is spent waiting between activities. In a number of cases, the wait time can consume a majority of the total time needed to complete a process. For example, some interlibrary loan departments found that moving away from a batch-oriented way of organizing things (in which a fair amount of time was spent waiting for the next step in the process) to a no-wait orientation significantly reduced the time it took to deliver the requested item into the hands of the customer.

The library might also examine its processes from the perspective of adding value. If a task or activity does not add value (or can be more appropriately done by someone else), then the task should be eliminated or reassigned. The goal of course is to understand the root causes of problems that may occur while the tasks and activities within a process are being performed.

The library must consider gathering data about its customers in new ways. The customer might be asked to provide additional information so that more personalized services can be offered. In addition, the library might collect more accurate information about who is using the library by requiring users to scan their library ID cards each time they enter and exit the library. Such data can then be combined with use of the collection information to generate more precise reports in terms of segmenting the potential population of users.[17]

> *One challenge associated with creating a culture of assessment in libraries relates to professional values. A profession that inherently believes that it is a "public good" does not feel the need to demonstrate outcomes and articulate impact. There is a deeply held and tacit assumption that the "good" is widely recognized and that the value of library service is universally appreciated. In the current environment of competition and of questioning every assumption, this deeply held value results in resistance to change and resistance to continuous improvement.*
> —Amos Alakos and Shelley Phipps[18]

Listening to the Voice of the Organization

Customers can usually articulate their information needs. Yet most customers are woefully ignorant about the ways in which libraries add value to the products and services that they offer their customers. Thus, a library must synthesize the needs of customers and respond in ways that will provide maximum value rather than simply responding to a customer request. Peter Senge has suggested that a learning organization is responsive to customers' needs in order to strengthen organizational learning and to position itself to serve customers in the future. In short, "a learning organization is one that is continually enhancing its capacity to create its future."[19] The disciplines practiced in a learning organization—systems thinking, shared vision, mental models, personal mastery, and team learning—can lead to a culture of assessment within a library.

Fostering the capacity of a library to create its future, question the current ways of doing things, and tap into the staff's creativity and commitment to provide high-quality services that meet the needs of its customers will help move the library in the direction of achieving its vision.

All of this requires leadership within the library that provides the support and infrastructure to assist staff members in assessing their contributions, experimenting, and helping move to the shared vision of the library's future.

One library with a culture of assessment, the University of Arizona library, has developed a Performance Effectiveness Management System (PEMS) to align the activities of the individual, unit, and the total library with the library's strategic goals and to provide measures that indicate success, progress, and the need for improvement.[20] The library has organized its staff into teams that are responsible for setting output, outcome, and specific quality measures to assess success. As a result of PEMS, the library has been able to decrease cycle time and increase the amount and quality of service, and has saved hundreds of thousands of dollars that have been reallocated to the purchase and upgrading of technology and the implementation of a competitive salary structure.

More than 20 years ago, Tom Peters and Bob Waterman found that top companies were "measurement-happy and performance-oriented."[21] Since that time, there has been an increasing amount of evidence to support their observation about the value of performance measurement. A more recent study found that top performing firms have a clarity of purpose and a vision of the future that are communicated throughout the organization and to interested stakeholders. These firms also measured what matters using a variety of metrics.[22]

Managers are not confronted with problems that are independent of each other, but with dynamic situations that consist of complex systems of changing problems that interact with each other. I call such situations messes. . . . Managers do not solve problems: they manage messes.

—Russell Ackoff[23]

Evaluation and assessment must become the norm in libraries. Assessment should be talked about and encouraged in staff meetings. Good assessment requires the active participation of staff at all levels, and different points of view are one of the foundations for a good culture of assessment. Such an environment allows the library to move from the use of traditional "internally focused" measures to the use of a combination of measures that will assist in revealing the value and impact of the library on its customers. Understanding, communicating, and measuring what matters from the customer's perspective is crucial in moving a library to an organization that embraces a culture of assessment. The library must be able to identify and communicate how it adds value to the lives of its users and the larger organizational context.

One quick way to assess the culture of assessment in your library is to answer the following questions. Does your library

- articulate a clear vision of the future that inspires employees?
- maintain consistency between words and actions?
- know what customers/users really care most about?
- know how well the library is doing to satisfy customers in terms of what the customers care most about?
- encourage the use of performance measures and analysis to assess problems and services?
- use resources efficiently? (*Are we doing things right?*)
- use resources effectively? (*Are we doing the right things?*)
- encourage employees to develop performance measurement skills?
- know how the library's policies and practices make the library "difficult to do business with?"
- demonstrate a constant pursuit of excellence?
- recruit talented people?
- learn from its mistakes?
- seize opportunities when they present themselves?
- work constantly to improve productivity and eliminate bureaucracy?
- communicate the value of your library to interested and key stakeholders?

Notes

1. Quoted in Arthur A. Thompson Jr. and A. J. Strickland III. *Crafting and Executing Strategy: Text and Readings*. New York: McGraw-Hill, 2001, 77.

2. Quoted in Andy Neely, Chris Adams, and Mike Kennerley. *The Performance Prism: The Scorecard for Measuring and Managing Business Success*. London: Prentice Hall, 2002, 158.

3. Heather Johnson. Strategic Planning for Modern Libraries. *Library Management*, 15 (1), 1994, 7–18.

4. Rowena Cullen. Does Performance Measurement Improve Organizational Effectiveness? A Postmodern Analysis. *Performance Measurement and Metrics*, 1 (1), August 1999, 9–30; Rowena Cullen. Does Performance Measurement Improve Organizational Effectiveness? A Postmodern Analysis, in

Proceedings of the 2nd Northumbria International Conference on Performance Measurement & Libraries & Information Services, September 7–11, 1997. Newcastle upon Tyne: Information North, 1998, 3–20.

5. Quoted in Thompson and Strickland, *Crafting and Executing Strategy*, 1.

6. Larry Nash White. Does Counting Count: An Evaluative Study of the Use and Impact of Performance Measurement in Florida Public Libraries. Ph.D. dissertation. Tallahassee: Florida State University, 2002.

7. Quoted in Thompson and Strickland, *Crafting and Executing Strategy*, 112.

8. Susan B. Barnard. Implementing Total Quality Management: A Model for Research Libraries. *Journal of Academic Librarianship*, 18, 1993, 57–70.

9. Roswitha Poll. Library Management with Cost Data. *World Library and Information Congress: 70th IFLA General Conference and Council, 22–27 August 2004, Buenos Aires, Argentina.* Available at http://www.ifla.org/IV/ifla70/papers/099e-Poll.pdf (accessed February 25, 2005).

10. Amos Lakos. Library Management Information Systems in the Client Server Environment: A Proposed New Model. *Proceedings of the 2nd Northumbria International Conference on Performance Measurement & Libraries & Information Services.* New Castle, England: University of Northumbria, 1998, 277–86.

11. Amos Lakos. Culture of Assessment as a Catalyst for Organizational Culture Change in Libraries. *Proceedings of the Fourth Northumbria International Conference on Performance Measurement in Libraries and Information Service, 12 to 16 August 2001.* New Castle, England: University of Northumbria, 2002, 311–20.

12. Choosing Our Futures. *College & Research Libraries*, 57 (3), May 1996, 225.

13. Shelley E. Phipps. Beyond Measuring Service Quality—Learning from the Voice of the Customers, the Staff, the Processes, and the Organization. *Proceeding of the ARL Measuring Service Quality Symposium, Washington DC, October 20–21, 2000.* Washington, DC: Association of Research Libraries, 2001.

14. Among the many articles about LibQUAL+, see Colleen Cook, Fred Heath, and Bruce Thompson. LibQUAL+: *One Instrument in the New Measures Toolbox*, 212. n.d. Available at http://www.arl.org/newsltr/212/libqual.html (accessed February 25, 2005); Colleen Cook and Bruce Thompson. Higher-Order Factor Analytic Perspectives on Users' Perceptions of Library Service Quality. *Library Information Science Research*, 22, 2000, 393–404; Colleen Cook and Bruce Thompson. Users' Hierarchical Perspectives on Library Service Quality: A "LibQUAL+"™ Study. *College and Research Libraries*, 62, 2001, 147–53; Colleen Cook and Fred Heath. Users' Perceptions of Library Services Quality: A "LibQUAL+" Qualitative Study. *Library Trends*, 49, 2001, 548–84; Bruce Thompson, Colleen Cook, and Russell L.

Thompson. Reliability and Structure of LibQUAL+ Scores: Measuring Perceived Library Service Quality. *Portal: Libraries and the Academy*, 2 (1), 2002, 3–12; Colleen Cook, Fred Heath, and Bruce Thompson. Score Norms for Improving Library Service Quality: A LibQUAL+ Study. *Portal: Libraries and the Academy*, 2 (1), 2002, 13–26; Fred Heath, Colleen Cook, Martha Kyrillidou, and Bruce Thompson. ARL Index and Other Validity Correlates of LibQUAL+ Scores. *portal: Libraries and the Academy*, 2 (1), 2002, 27–42; Carolyn A. Snyder. Measuring Library Service Quality with a Focus on the LibQUAL+ Project: An Interview with Fred Heath. *Library Administration & Management*, 16 (1), Winter 2002, 4–7.

15. Marianne Broadbent and Hans Lofgren. Information Delivery: Identifying Priorities, Performance and Value, in OPAC and Beyond. *Victorian Association for Library Automation 6th Biennial Conference and Exhibition. 11–13 November 1991, Hilton on the Park, Melbourne, Australia,* 185–215; Marianne Broadbent. Demonstrating Information Service Value to Your Organization. *Proceedings of the IOLIM Conference,* 16, 1992, 65–83; Marianne Broadbent and Hans Lofgren. *Priorities, Performance and Benefits: An Exploratory Study of Library and Information Units.* Melbourne, Australia: CIRCIT Ltd. and ACLIS, 1991.

16. Susan Edwards and Mairead Browne. Quality in Information Services: Do Users and Librarians Differ in Their Expectations. *Library & Information Science Review*, 17, 1995, 163–82.

17. Emma Robinson. Studying User Satisfaction: Who Do It? How to Do It? Where Next? One Library's Experience. *The New Review of Academic Librarianship*, 1, 1995, 179–85.

18. Creating a Culture of Assessment: A Catalyst for Organizational Change. *Portal: Libraries and the Academy*, 4 (3), July 2004, 350.

19. Peter M. Senge. *The Fifth Discipline: The Art and Practice of the Learning Organization.* New York: Doubleday, 1990, 14.

20. Carla Stoffle. Creating a Culture of Assessment: The University of Arizona Experience. *ARL Bimonthly Report*, 230/231, October/December 2003. Available at: http://www.arl.org/newsltr/2301/cultureaz.html (accessed February 25, 2005).

21. Thomas J. Peters and Robert H. Waterman Jr. *In Search of Excellence: Lesson's from American's Best-Run Companies.* New York: Harper & Row, 1982.

22. Howard M. Armitage and Vijay M. Jog. Creating & Measuring Shareholder Value: A Canadian Perspective. *Ivey Business Journal*, 63 (5), July/August 1999, 75–81.

23. Quoted in Donald A. Schon. *The Reflective Practitioner: How Professionals Think in Action.* New York: Basic Books, 1983, 16.

Chapter 10

Tools for Managing the Library

Culture changes only after you have altered people's actions, after the new behavior produces some group benefit for a period of time, and after people see the connection between the new actions and the performance improvement.—John Kotter[1]

Four management tools—strategic planning, mission and vision statements, benchmarking, and customer satisfaction measurement—are the most frequently used worldwide, according to a survey of managers.[2] Other tools, such as customer segmentation, identifying core competencies, reengineering, the balanced scorecard, and total quality management, while helpful, are used slightly less frequently.

Historically, budgets have played an obviously important role in controlling what products and services are delivered to the library's customers. However, rather than being a tool for the successful implementation of strategies and plans, the budget has taken on a life of its own. The reality for most libraries is that the budget process is controlled and structured in such a way as to preclude a careful reassessment of the library's vision, goals, and strategies. In this regard, one has only to note the failure of such alternative budgetary process as zero-based budgeting and program planning budgeting to gain popularity or regular use.[3] Budgeting has become a process for small incremental increases or decreases in the library's budget, depending on the availability of funding within the larger organizational context. For public, academic, and school libraries, the process can be "energized" by politics, as many departments, special interests, and individuals struggle for a bigger piece of the pie. And the same annual budget struggles are often found within the special library arena.

There are a variety of different types and methods for preparing the budget, including the following:

- *Line-item:* This budget is the most frequently used. A line detailing the requested funds represents each category within the budget. Broad categories of expenditures may be divided into smaller divisions and further subdivisions. Typically the funding decision makers will pre-establish a maximum total incremental increase of the forthcoming budget compared to the existing year's budget. The focus is on the monetary inputs that the library will use to deliver its services. This type of budget has limited utility as a planning tool.

- *Program:* A budget is prepared using service areas, for example, circulation, reference, collection, and so forth, and a line-item budget is then prepared for each area. This type of budget is useful for planning since there is a link between inputs and outputs but does require a bit more work to proportionally allocate some costs across the service areas.

- *Performance:* This type of budget, sometimes called a Planning Programming Budgeting System (PPBS), adds the use of performance measures to a program budget. Such an approach requires setting goals for each service area, considering alternative methods for achieving those goals, and selecting a set of performance measures that are used to assess actual performance.

- *Zero-based:* This is a "bottom-up" approach to budgeting and requires each department to build a budget for diffcrent levels of activity (from minimal or zero cost to ideal funding). Each budget must specify goals, levels of activity that can be supported, and performance measures that will be used to assess overall performance. Each budget is then evaluated and ranked and the availability of funds determines what will be done in the coming year. This approach is time-consuming, complex, and rarely used today.

- *Priority-based:* Priority-based budgeting (PBB) requires managers to establish the minimum level (and cost) of the service to meet essential requirements and then identify successive increments of costs (and benefits) using a 10-point rating system. This allows the funding decision makers to know the service consequences of providing funding at a specific level.

Involving knowledgeable analysts and garnering a seasoned veteran of the budgetary process will assist the library in preparing and critiquing the library's budget. In addition, the library director should make sure that she is attuned to the organization's top decision makers so that the library's strategies and goals are closely aligned with those of the larger organization.

Organizations that focus on strategies have found that strategic planning actually occurs informally on a year-round basis. A more formal strategic planning process that occurs over a short period of time typically precedes the budget cycle. Some public organizations have found that using "entrepreneurial budgeting" will allow budgets to be linked to strategies the results of which managers are then held accountable for, and it can assist in promoting a new kind of entrepreneurial culture.[4]

Performance Measures

> *Performance measurement is to reinvention what navigation is to exploration. In both instances, we greatly reduce the risk of failure if we chart our course in advance, take our bearings and measure progress frequently, and make timely corrections when we blow off course. The better the navigational performance measurement system, the more likely we are to succeed in our mission.*
> —Michael Campbell[5]

The use of performance measures is not an end in itself but rather a means to improve operations and services and for reporting to various stakeholders, provided the appropriate measures are used. It is possible to consider the variety of potential measures as forming a hierarchy, as shown in Figure 10.1 (p. 112). The library can utilize a variety of input, process, output, and outcome or impact performance measures.[6]

The key to communicating how effective the library is to its customers is to actively involve the various stakeholders, especially the funding decision makers, in determining what information they would like to know about the library. In particular, asking these individuals what questions about the library they would like answered is very important to have a better understanding of what issues and perspectives are important to them individually and collectively. With this understanding in hand, it is then possible to identify a set of performance measures that will have maximum impact in communicating value.

Neil McLean and Clare Wilde have revised and expanded upon the evaluation model originally developed by Orr (see Figure 10.2, p. 113). This revised model clearly demonstrates the wide variety of measures that can be selected by a library and differentiates the activities in the library that are performed by staff to prepare materials for use (Technical Processes) from the activities performed by staff that interact with the users of the library (Public Processes). Remember that a performance measure is simply a quantitative description of a specific process or activity and the measure requires some context and analysis in order to understand its underlying meaning.

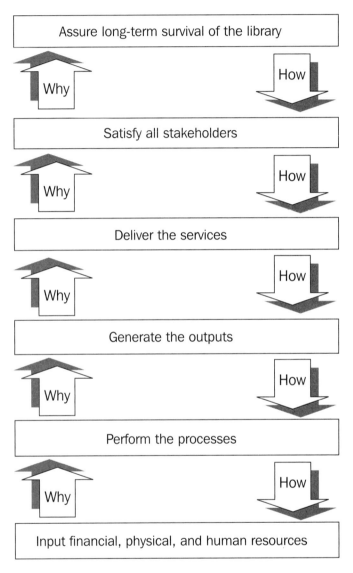

Figure 10.1. Hierarchy of Performance Measures

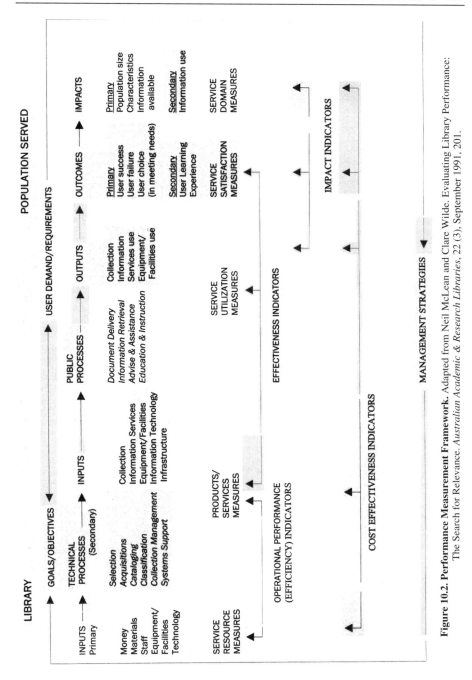

Figure 10.2. Performance Measurement Framework. Adapted from Neil McLean and Clare Wilde. Evaluating Library Performance: The Search for Relevance. *Australian Academic & Research Libraries*, 22 (3), September 1991, 201.

Ultimately the success of a library director and of the library's budget is a political judgment on the part of the various stakeholders, particularly the funding decision makers, and of the citizens themselves (especially if they are called upon to vote for an increased tax levy) about the utility and value of the library to its customers and the larger organizational context.

This is accomplished by first identifying the strategies that the library will be using to deliver the services it has selected that will be most responsive to its customers. Then the library needs to identify that set of input, process, output, and outcome measures that will reflect the contribution of the library to individuals and to the larger organizational context, as shown in Figure 10.3. Once these measures have been selected, it is important to ensure that the collection and use of the measures are clearly understood by all library staff members. To achieve the library's vision of the future, goals are set for each measure (usually interim goals are also established). Finally, the performance measures are collected and distributed to all staff members and stakeholders on a quarterly basis. The measures are then discussed in regular library management and staff meetings so that the importance of the measures becomes clear. Any corrective actions, if any, can then be discussed and planned.

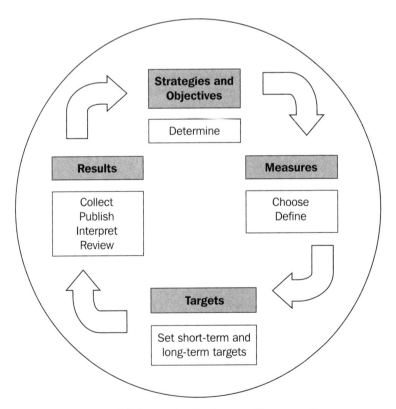

Figure 10.3. Approach to Performance Measurement

WHY MEASURE PERFORMANCE?

If you don't measure results, you can't tell success from failure.

If you can't see success, you can't reward it.

If you can't reward success, you're probably rewarding failure.

If you can't see success, you can't learn from it.

If you can't recognize failure, you can't correct it.

If you can demonstrate results, you can win public support.

—David Osborne and Ted Gaebler[7]

It is also important to select performance measures of activities and services over which the library has complete control. An effective performance measurement system has the following attributes:

- *Clarity of Purpose:* The audience for whom the measures are being collected and analyzed is clearly stated. Those in the target audience should readily understand the indicators.

- *Focus:* The measures chosen should reflect the service objectives of the library.

- *Alignment:* The performance measures should be synchronized with the goals and objectives of the library. Too many libraries routinely collect too many statistics and performance measures that then are casually ignored.

- *Balance:* The measures that are selected for use should present a balanced view of the library and its overall performance. Some of the measures should include outcomes and the user perspective. Measures describe different characteristics of performance:

  - *Absolute/Relative*: An absolute measure is one that can stand on its own. A relative performance measure is compared to the same measure in other "similar" libraries.

  - *Process/Function Oriented:* A process measure looks at the various tasks and activities that comprise a functional activity, for example, cataloging. A functional measure takes a broader view.

  - *Performance/Diagnostic:* Some performance measures are designed to measure the achievements of a particular service, while others are gathered to assist in analyzing a process or activity with the goal of improving the activity.

- *Objective/Subjective:* Objective measures reflect a specific activity, for example, circulation, while a subjective measure reflects an opinion or observation by a trained professional, for example, adequacy and depth of a collection, or by customers, for example, satisfaction surveys. Sometimes objective data are referred to as "hard measures," while subjective data have been called "soft measures."

- *Direct/Indirect:* A direct indicator measures a specific activity (circulation). An indirect indicator provides an estimate for an activity (the number of online catalog searches is used as a surrogate to estimate number of people who used the online catalog, for example, 2.5 searches = 1 person).

- *Leading/Lagging:* A leading performance measure provides some advance warning that another activity will increase or decrease. A lagging measure reflects actual performance, for example, circulation.

- *Social/Economic:* Combinations of social and economic outcome measures can be used.

• *Regular Refinement:* The performance indicators that are collected should be periodically reviewed to ensure that their continued use provides the library with real value. In some cases, a new measure should be introduced and another be dropped.

• *Vigorous Performance Indicators:* Each performance measure should be clearly defined and relevant. The data collected should be unambiguous and not open to manipulation. Readily available statistics, such as the number of Web site hits, are often more dangerous than useful.

The selection of a particular performance measure should be carefully considered from a number of perspectives. A series of questions that should be answered for each measure are provided in Table 10.1.

Table 10.1 Measures Definition Template*

Measure:
- What should the measure be called?
- Does the title explain what the measure is?
- Is it a title that everyone will understand?
- Is it clear why the measure is important?

Purpose:
- Why is the measure being introduced?
- What is the aim/intention of the measure?
- What behaviors should the measure encourage?

Relates to:
- Which other measures does this one closely relate to?
- What specific strategies or initiatives does it support?

Metric/Formula:
- How can this dimension of performance be measured?
- Can the formula be defined in mathematical terms?
- Is the metric/formula clear?
- Does the metric/formula explain exactly what data are required?
- What behavior is the metric/formula intended to induce?
- Are there any other behaviors that the metric/formula should induce?
- Are there any dysfunctional behaviors that might be induced?
- Is the scale being used appropriately?
- How accurate will the data generated be?
- Are the data accurate enough?
- If an average is being used, how much data will be lost?
- Is the loss of "granularity" acceptable?
- Would it be better to measure the speed of performance?

Target level(s):
- What level of performance is desirable?
- How long will it take to reach this level of performance?
- Are interim milestone targets required?
- How do these target levels of performance compare with competitors?
- How good is the competition currently?
- How fast is the competition improving?

Frequency:
- How often should this measure be taken?
- How often should this measure be reported?
- Is this frequency sufficient to track the effect of actions taken to improve?

Source of data:
- Where will the data to track this measure come from?

Who measures:
- Who—by name, function or external agency—is actually responsible for collecting, collating, and analyzing these data?

Who acts on the data (owner):
- Who—by name or function—is actually responsible for initiating actions and ensuring that performance along this dimension improves?

What do they do:
- How exactly will the measure owner use these data?
- What actions will they take to ensure that performance along this dimension improves?

*Adapted from Andy Neely, Chris Adams, and Mike Kennerley. *The Performance Prism: The Scorecard for Measuring and Managing Business Success.* London: Prentice Hall, 2002, 37.

The selection, collection, and sharing of performance measures are designed to provide improved services as well as increased accountability by informing all of the library's stakeholders of how well the library is actually doing. The library might want to consider grouping the measures into three or four categories, as shown in Figure 10.4.

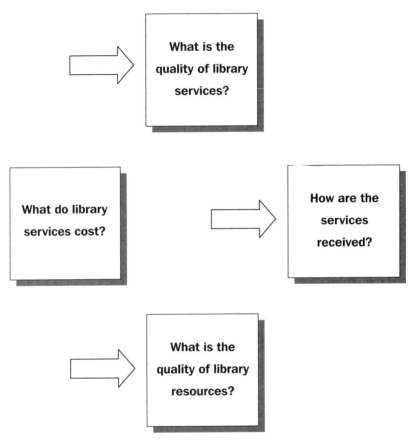

Figure 10.4. Public Library Performance Measures

Among the measures that are reported to stakeholders there should be a balance among input, process (efficiency), output, and outcome measures. Possible performance measures include the following:

- What do library services cost?
    - Library budget expenditures per capita
    - Materials expenditures per capita
    - Proportion of materials expenditures spent on electronic resources

- Cost of technical services per item added to the collection
- Cost benefit analysis or return-on-investment (ROI)

• What is the quality of library services?

- Open hours per week
- Number of public access computers
- Reliability of the computer network and systems
- Accuracy of reference question responses
- Social benefits for each service response
- Economic benefits for each service response
- "Mystery shopper" ratings

• What is the quality of the collection and access to electronic resources?

- Immediate availability of collection materials
- Number of titles/volumes added to the collection
- Percent of collection added in last 5 years, 10 years
- Number of full-text periodicals accessible using electronic resources
- Proportion of collection added in last five years that has been used

• How are the services accepted?

- Market penetration (active users as a percent of total population)
- Circulation per capita
- Reference questions per capita
- User satisfaction survey
- Time saved by customers
- Estimated value of services provided

These measures are meant to be illustrative rather than prescriptive. And it is important to provide some context for each of these measures so that library stakeholders will know whether a market penetration figure, for example, is better than, about the same as, or less than other comparable libraries. In addition, it might be illuminating to provide information about the set of performance measures over the course of the last four to five years so that people will have a better idea about possible trends. An example of the way in which a library might present this information about a set of performance measures is shown in Figure 10.5 (pp. 120–22). This approach relies on presenting the information in graphical form so that trends are immediately apparent.

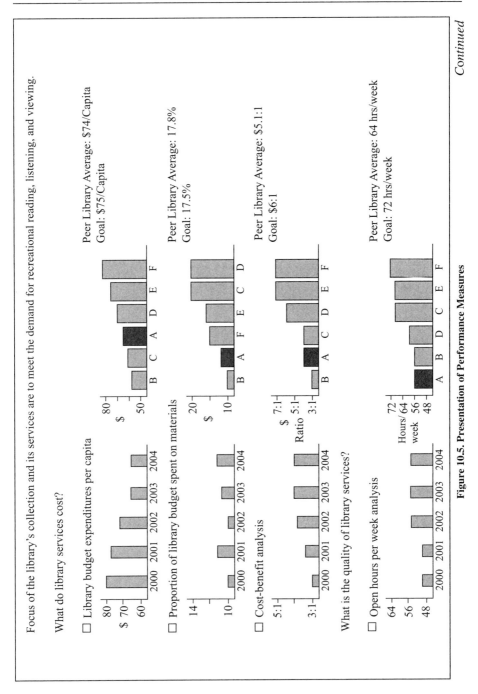

Figure 10.5. Presentation of Performance Measures

Continued

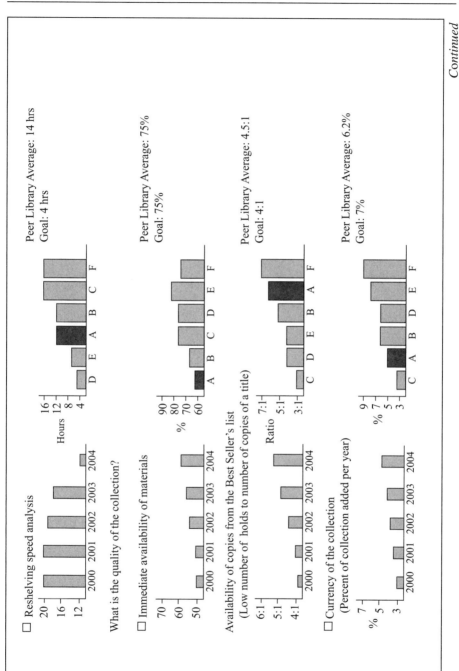

Continued

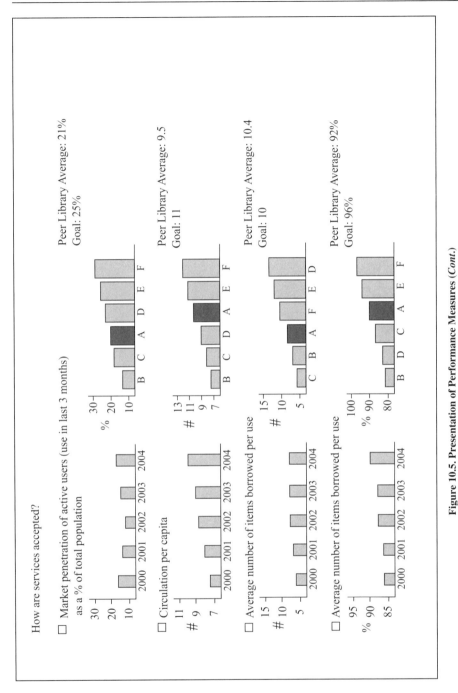

Figure 10.5. Presentation of Performance Measures (*Cont.*)

An alternative presentation of performance measures is shown in Table 10.2. This particular arrangement reflects the different viewpoints that can be employed for a particular library service. It is important to note that this approach requires the library to articulate in writing an objective that states an improvement for a specific set of users. This approach can be expanded by subdividing the "outcomes" column into three columns: initial, intermediate, and long-term outcomes.

The Balanced Scorecard

One approach to communicating value and performance that has taken on an increasingly important role in for-profit, nonprofit, and governmental organizations is the use of the balanced scorecard.

Responding to the criticisms of the late 1980s that accountants and the typical organization's annual report provided a narrow, backward-looking or lagging financial perspective and thus was not helpful in assisting the reader in understanding the overall health and performance of the organization, Robert Kaplan and David Norton suggested through a series of articles and books that the balanced scorecard provided a broader perspective.[8]

The process of developing a balanced scorecard is based on the premise that all of the performance measures that are selected are linked to the strategies that have been selected by the organization. The scorecard approach is based on answering four basic questions, each defining a perspective of the library's value:

- How do customers and stakeholders see the library? (Customer perspective)

- What must the library excel at? (Internal perspective)

- Can the library continue to improve and create value? (Innovation and learning perspective)

- How does the public library look to stakeholders? (Financial perspective)

Table 10.2. Potential Performance Measures

Service Area	Objective	Input	Output	Efficiency	Service Quality	Outcomes
Lending of popular books, audio, and video materials	To increase the percent of the potential customer base who borrow materials at least 4 times a year from X% to Y%	Budget of staff that supports lending of popular materials	Total number of items loaned per year (Circulation)	Cost per item borrowed	Availability rate	Cost-benefit ratio
		Materials acquisitions budget	Circulation per Capita	Cost to order, receive, and process materials to make shelf ready	Number of days to get a copy of a book on the best seller's list	Customer satisfaction
		Materials acquisitions budget as a % of the total budget	Collection turnover rate			The borrowed material assists an individual find a job, do their job faster and more accurately, saves money, and so forth
Provide access to electronic full-text journals	To increase the percent of customers who gain access to electronic full-text journals from X% to Y%	Budget for electronic full-text journals	Number of individuals who use electronic full-text journals	Cost of electronic full-text journals per title	Time when electronic full-text journals are not accessible (downtime—as a % of 168 hours per week)	Cost-benefit ratio
		Budget for electronic full-text journals as a % of the total budget	Number of electronic full-text journals titles accessed	Cost of electronic full-text journals per user	Response time to log on to service	Customer satisfaction
			Number of electronic full-text journals articles downloaded	Cost of electronic full-text journals per capita	Response time to download a 1MB file with a 56 Kb modem	The percent of the community that gains access to the electronic full-text journals at least 4 times a year

Service Area	Objective	Input	Output	Efficiency	Service Quality	Outcomes
Reference services	To increase the percent of customers who use reference services at least 4 times a year from X% to Y%	Budget of reference staff Reference materials acquisitions budget	Number of reference questions answered (directional questions are excluded) Number of individuals who attend an information literacy class	Cost of reference services per question answered Cost of reference services per capita	Accuracy of reference answers Completeness of reference answers	Customer satisfaction The percent of the community that uses the reference service at least 4 times a year
Children's Services	To increase the percent of the community who use the children's services at least 4 times a year from X% to Y%	Budget of children's services staff Children's materials acquisitions budget Children's materials acquisitions budget as a percent of the total materials acquisitions budget	Circulation of children's materials Circulation of children's materials per capita Children's materials turnover rate Attendance at children's activities—story hours	Cost per item borrowed Cost to order, receive, and processes materials Cost of children's services staff per capita Cost of children's services staff per story hour attendee	Availability rate Number of days to get a copy of a children's book on the hold (request) list	Cost-benefit ratio Customer satisfaction The percent of the community that borrows children's materials at least 4 times a year The percent of the community that attends children's activities at least 4 times a year

Providing a set of performance measures for each perspective simultaneously lets the organization see "whether improvements in one area may have been achieved at the expense of another." Using this approach means that the library can consider disparate elements of the competitive agenda such as becoming more customer oriented, shortening response times, improving collection quality, emphasizing teamwork, and developing totally new services altogether.

Viewing a variety of performance indicators that are focused on the four perspectives allows management to take a broader view. The library does not just pursue circulation, or customer satisfaction, or expenditures on fiction in isolation. Rather, the scorecard provides a vehicle that allows the management team and library staff members to see how their combined actions are reflected in the performance indicators considered as a uniform set.[9] An overview of the balanced scorecard is shown in Figure 10.6.

- *Customer Perspective (Users):* Customer concerns tend to fall into four categories: time, quality, performance and service, and cost. A variety of customer-focused measures can be employed, including customer satisfaction (although customer satisfaction surveys must be used cautiously in a library setting due to their positively skewed results). The strategies selected by the library should be designed to answer two questions: Who are our customers? What value does the library provide to them?

- *Internal Perspective:* Managers should focus on the critical internal operations that enable them to satisfy customer needs. This part of the scorecard looks at the processes and competencies in which a library must excel. In addition to productivity measures, technological capability and introduction of new ideas to improve an existing service or a new service might be addressed.

- *Innovation and Learning Perspective:* This looks at the library's ability to grow, learn, develop, and introduce new services. It focuses on measures such as the quality of the existing infrastructure, organizational culture, and the improvement of library staff member skills. Measures in this perspective are really enablers for the other perspectives. A library will typically identify and create new measures for this perspective.

- *Financial Perspective:* In the arena of an academic, public, school, government, or nonprofit library, financial measures such as profitability are not directly relevant. However, regardless of the type of library, it can, and must, demonstrate that it makes effective use of the funding that is provided.

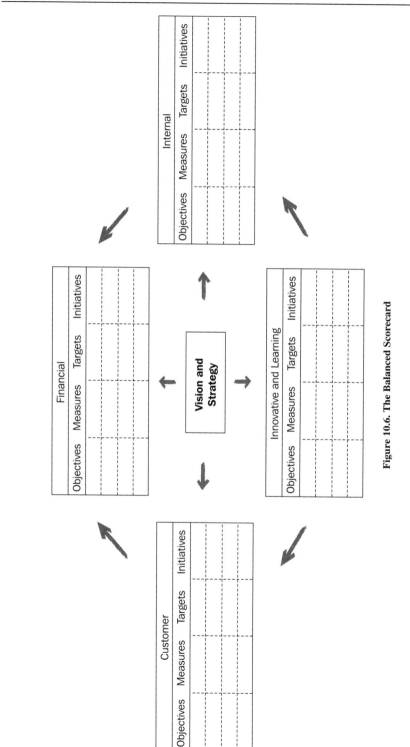

Figure 10.6. The Balanced Scorecard

In the for-profit arena, the assumption is that the innovative perspective (dealing with infrastructure and the quality of staff) will create a more efficient operation (internal perspective). The combination of staff, infrastructure, and internal operations will lead to products and services that will be more appealing to customers. The customers are then going to purchase more products and services, leading to better financial results (financial perspective).

Once measures for each perspective have been identified, the ultimate target and interim goals for each target are selected. One of the challenges is to establish goals that are a bit of a stretch for the library to achieve and yet are based on considering the current performance of the processes used to deliver the results. Arbitrary goals and targets invite fear, frustration, and distortion of the performance measures being collected. One helpful technique is to create process charts that reveal the existing performance.[10]

The resulting scorecard assists a library in translating its vision and strategies by providing a framework that helps communicate the library's strategy through the objectives and measures chosen.

Since traditional measurement systems sprang from the finance function, the performance measurement systems have historically had a control bias. That is, traditional performance measurement systems specify the particular actions they want employees to take and then measure to see whether the employees have in fact taken those actions. In that way, the accounting systems try to control behavior.

The balanced scorecard, on the other hand, puts strategy and vision, not control, at the center. It establishes goals but assumes that people will adopt whatever behavior and take whatever actions are necessary to help achieve those goals. The goal is to minimize the gap that exists between the mission and performance measures. The focus should be on what the library intends to achieve, not the programs and initiatives that are being implemented to achieve the library's vision.

The strength of the balanced scorecard is that the selected performance measures are those, or should be those, that will reflect the strategies embraced by the library. One of the crucial steps is to develop a strategy map that clearly identifies the cause-and-effect relationships of each strategy to the other perspectives.[11] A strategy map is a one-page picture of the library's strategy or strategies that articulates the objectives from the four perspectives. The strategy map thus becomes an anchor with which the library can manage and motivate its staff members.

For example, a library might want to improve the quality and variety of services available to its online customers so that these services are similar to those received by customers who visit the library. This might require improved technology skill levels for some staff, upgraded technology infrastructures, a change in existing procedures to provide some services, and a larger budget allocation for capital expenses and training. The end result, it is hoped, will be more satisfied online customers. The challenge? Selecting performance measures that reflect the underlying strategy for each perspective. The result will be a series of interconnected objectives and measures flowing through each perspective.

A great many libraries will measure progress in achieving milestones of their annual initiatives. Initiatives should exist to assist the library in achieving its strategic objectives. The initiatives are the means and not the end. Strategy and its associated performance measures should focus on what output and outcomes the library intends to achieve, not what programs and initiatives are being implemented.

The balanced scorecard is a useful framework that provides the focal point when a library is trying to draw up its performance measures. The system is based on the understanding that no *single* measure can focus attention on all of the critical areas of service. And the set of performance measures that are selected must work together coherently to reflect the achievement of the overall goals of the library.

> *Success for nonprofits should be measured by how effectively and efficiently they meet the needs of their constituencies. Financial considerations can play an enabling or constraining role but will rarely be the primary objective.*
>
> —Robert S. Kaplan[12]

A Library Scorecard

Robert Kaplan has suggested an alternative scorecard for nonprofit organizations (see Figure 10.7, p. 130).[13] Rather than using the original balanced scorecard with its four perspectives that were created for for-profit firms, a revised balanced scorecard may be more appropriate for academic, public, government, school, and nonprofit libraries. In addition to a reorganized structure, the library balanced scorecard introduces an additional perspective—*information resources*, as shown in Figure 10.8 (p. 130). These information resources comprise the library's physical collection, the access to electronic databases subscribed to by the library, as well as obtaining resources from other sources, such as libraries through interlibrary loan and/or a document delivery service.

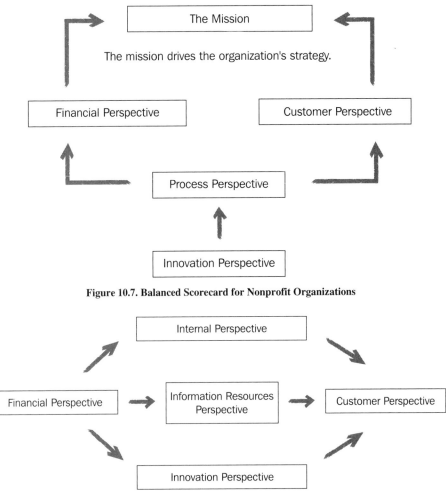

Figure 10.7. Balanced Scorecard for Nonprofit Organizations

Figure 10.8. The Library Scorecard

The library scorecard model suggests that the financial resources provided to the library are used to provide the information resources and staff (which uses a variety of processes and procedures measured using the internal perspective), build the infrastructure, and provide staff training. All of these are combined to provide services to users (the customer perspective).

Performance Prism

Somewhat similar to the balanced scorecard, the performance prism was developed in England by a team led by Andy Neely and consists of five interrelated perspectives on performance:[14]

- *Stakeholder Satisfaction:* Who are our key stakeholders, and what do they want and need?

- *Stakeholder Contribution:* What do we want and need from our stakeholders on a reciprocal basis?

- *Strategies:* What strategies do we need to put in place to satisfy the wants and needs of stakeholders while satisfying our own requirements?

- *Processes:* What processes do we need to put in place to enable us to execute our strategies?

- *Capabilities:* What capabilities do we need to put in place to allow us to operate our processes?

These five perspectives provide a broad, comprehensive framework for thinking about organizational performance. Figure 10.9 illustrates these five basic perspectives on performance management.

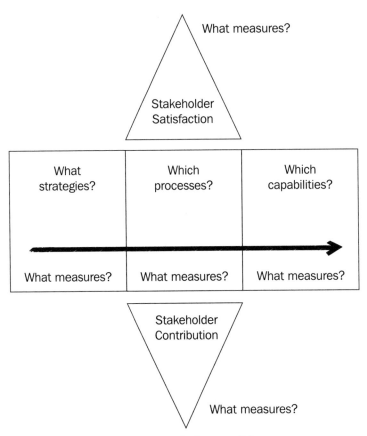

Figure 10.9 The Performance Prism

Compared to the balanced scorecard, the inclusion of the "stakeholder satisfaction" perspective provides a broader view. Stakeholders include funding decision makers, suppliers, and partners as well as customers and employees. Another unique perspective is that of "strategies." This perspective focuses on what strategies are chosen by the library to achieve its vision.

Capabilities are the combination of people, technology, and infrastructure, factors that enable the organization's ability to execute its processes. The obvious question for this perspective is, what are the key capabilities to operate our processes?

The "stakeholder contribution" facet recognizes that various stakeholders make contributions in the form of budgets, support, and in other ways. Employees, for example, are looking for a secure place to work with good working conditions, a decent salary, and recognition. In return the organization wants its employees to be responsible when working, offer suggestions, develop their skills, and remain loyal.

The selection of performance measures that are linked to these five perspectives assists the library in best managing its resources to better meet the needs of its customers.

He who stops being better stops being good.
—Oliver Cromwell[15]

Three Rs of Performance

Yet another potential management tool is the "Three Rs of Performance."[16] This tool provides a balanced approach to performance management by providing a strategic and comprehensive context for decision making (see Figure 10.10).

Resources refer to both the amount of time, money, and/or energy exerted as well as the type of resources used. Types of resources include capital and people, skill types, and competencies required of staff, as well as the physical and spatial location of resources. It is important to understand the total resources committed to a service, program, or the entire library system as well as the key characteristics of the resources. Tools such as ROI and net present value (NPV) were developed to optimize resource utilization by maximizing the financial returns.

Reach refers to the breadth and depth of influence over which available resources are spread. Physical (spatial) reach is one dimension, as well as the type of customers the library wishes to reach. For many services and programs, reach goals relate to the number and extent of clients served. Michael Porter, the strategy guru, and others have emphasized that an organization needs to focus on market share. As competition becomes an increasing concern, market share becomes an important indicator of success.

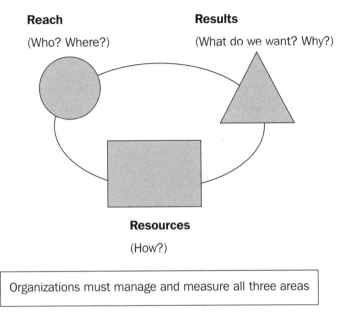

Reach

(Who? Where?)

Results

(What do we want? Why?)

Resources

(How?)

Organizations must manage and measure all three areas

Figure 10.10. The Three Rs of Performance

Results refer to the impact on the groups of customers reached by the resources used. Desired results usually indicate the attainment of a desired outcome for the individual or the larger community being served. Often an organization will focus on service quality as a means to achieve better results. Value has been added when the results are desirable from the customer's perspective. Customers may express themselves by indicating higher levels of satisfaction.

Using a balanced scorecard based on the "Three Rs of Performance," as shown in Figure 10.11, allows a library to better understand the tradeoffs inherent in decision making and provides a means for strategic and operational planning while monitoring progress toward achieving specific goals.

Performance Area	Indicators/Measures	Systems
Resources	Investment in core competencies Cost by service offered	Cost accounting
Reach	Clients served by segment Clients served by target population	Client tracking
Results	Service quality Economic benefits Social benefits	Client surveys
Key ratios: —Cost per client served —Cost per result (service)		

Figure 10.11. Generic Three Rs Scorecard

Since resources, reach, and results are all linked together, the best approach would seem to be to optimize among them in choosing goals and strategies rather than focusing on one of the three Rs. The value of using the three Rs is that it helps the top management team of an organization as well as the stakeholders understand the tradeoffs associated with a particular decision. Not surprisingly, most organizations focus most of their efforts on reporting measures concerning resources.

Summary

> Changing something implies not just learning something new but unlearning something that is already there and possibly in the way. What most learning theories and models overlook are the dynamics of unlearning, of overcoming resistance to change. They assume that if you can get a clear enough vision of a positive future, this is motivation enough to get new learning started.
>
> —Edgar Schein[17]

The value of using a tool such as the balanced scorecard, the performance prism, or the three Rs scorecard is that it facilitates the communication process with a variety of stakeholders that are important to the library. In particular, it affords the library director the opportunity of determining what measures are going to be of value to the library's funding decision makers. More important, it provides a vehicle for the library to identify those strategies that it will use to most effectively serve the needs of its customers. Having identified the strategies, the library can then select a set of performance measures to track that are linked to the selected strategies. Performance measures track customer satisfaction and the processes that lead to those results. Thus, it is important for the library to utilize performance measures, since what you measure is what you get.[18]

Reinforcing the reality that no tool is a panacea, a recent study of organizations using a balanced scorecard found the following:

- About one-third reported that their resource allocation is now in line with strategy.

- Only 12 percent said that their planning and budgeting processes have improved.

- Some 31 percent reported that they use the scorecard to improve strategic learning.

- Only 10 percent agreed that the use of the scorecard improved their bottom line.[19]

Organizational performance is driven by people and the processes they use to deliver services. Overlaying a new management tool without carefully considering the value and utility of the library's existing organizational structure may mean that all of the potential benefits will not be achieved. Worse, the existing organizational structure and the traditions embraced by the culture within the library may be setting up a project to implement a scorecard for failure. Thus, it may be necessary to change the existing organizational structure when implementing a scorecard that focuses on outcomes. It is important to remember that scorecards are about providing an overview and balance about the library and not primarily as a collection of separate performance measures.

> *Change only happens when "creative tension" is created. Creative tension comes from seeing where we want to be, our "vision," and telling the truth about where we are now, our "current reality."*
> —Peter Senge[20]

At the conclusion of the strategic planning process, the library director, top management team, and interested stakeholders should be able to answer the following questions:

- What are the mission, vision, and values of the library?

- What is the business of this library, and what is the strategic orientation of the library? Or, what are the strategies that are being used to reach the library's vision?

- Who are the customers served, and how does the library add value?

- What is the nature of the strategy formation process in the library, who participates in it, and where are the strategies documented?

- What are the critical success factors or business drivers for the library?

- How do the library's services and products relate to each of the business drivers?

- Who are the key decision makers for the library?

- What are the library's service and product priorities of the key stakeholders?

- What is the perception of the key stakeholders of performance and benefit for the library's services and products?

- What performance measures are used to track the success of the strategies being employed by the library?

- Is the library striving to create a culture of assessment by training staff to use analysis and statistical techniques to solve problems?

- Has the library considered using some form of a balanced scorecard or other management tool to facilitate communicating the value of the library to key stakeholders?

Notes

1. John Kotter. *Leading Change*. Boston: Harvard Business School Press, 1996, 156.

2. Darrell Rigby. Management Tools and Techniques: A Survey. *California Management Review*, 43 (2), Winter 2001, 139–60.

3. Jeremy Hope and Robin Fraser. *Beyond Budgeting: How Managers Can Break Free from the Annual Performance Trap*. Boston: Harvard Business School Press, 2003.

4. David Osborne and Ted Gaebler. *Reinventing Government: How the Entrepreneurial Spirit Is Transforming the Public Sector*. New York: Addison-Wesley, 1992.

5. Michael Campbell. *Building Results: New Tools for an Age of Discovery in Government*. Washington, DC: Council of Governors Policy, May 1, 1994.

6. Jennifer Cram. Performance Management, Measurement and Reporting in a Time of Information-Centred Change. *The Australian Library Journal*, 45 (3), August 1996, 225–38.

7. Osborne and Gaebler, *Reinventing Government*.

8. Robert S. Kaplan and David P. Norton. *Strategy Maps: Converting Intangible Assets Into Tangible Outcomes*. Boston: Harvard Business School Press, 2004; Robert S. Kaplan and David P. Norton. *The Strategy-Focused Organization: How Balanced Scorecard Companies Thrive in the New Business Environment*. Boston: Harvard Business School Press, 2001; Robert S. Kaplan and David P. Norton. *The Balanced Scorecard: Translating Strategy into Action*. Boston: Harvard Business School Press, 1996; Robert S. Kaplan and David P. Norton. The Balanced Scorecard—Measures That Drive Performance. *Harvard Business Review*, January–February 1992, 71–79.

9. Charles Birch. *Future Success: A Balanced Approach to Measuring and Improving Success in Your Organization*. New York: Prentice-Hall, 2000; Mark Graham Brown. *Winning Score: How to Design and Implement Organizational Scorecards*. Portland, OR: Productivity, 2000.

10. Larry B. Weinstein and Joseph F. Castellano. Benchmarking and Stretch Targets Are Often Adopted to Support the Balanced Scorecard. But Do They Do What Is Necessary to Make Scorecard Effective? Using Statistical Process Control Might Be More Effective. *CMA Management*, April 2004, 19–22.

11. Robert S. Kaplan and David P. Norton. *Strategy Maps: Converting Intangible Assets into Tangible Outcomes.* Boston: Harvard Business School Press, 2004.

12. Robert S. Kaplan. Strategic Performance Measurement and Management in Nonprofit Organizations. *Nonprofit Management & Leadership*, 11 (3), Spring 2001, 353–70.

13. Kaplan, Strategic Performance Measurement and Management in Nonprofit Organizations, 353–70.

14. Andy Neely, Chris Adams, and Mike Kennerley. *The Performance Prism: The Scorecard for Measuring and Managing Business Success.* London: Prentice Hall, 2002; Andy Neely and Chris Adams. The Performance Prism Perspective. *Journal of Cost Management*, 15 (1), January/February 2001, 7–15; Andy Neely, Chris Adams, and Paul Crowe. The Performance Prism in Practice. *Measuring Business Excellence*, 5 (2), 2001, 6–12; Andy Neely, John Mills, Ken Platts, Mike Gregory, and Huw Richards. Realizing Strategy Through Measurement. *International Journal of Operations & Production Management*, 14 (3), 1994, 140–52.

15. Oliver Cromwell Quotes. Available at http://www.brainyquote.com/quotes/authors/o/oliver_cromwell.html (accessed February 25, 2005).

16. Steve Montague. *The Three Rs of Performance: Core Concepts for Planning, Measurement, and Management.* Ottawa, Canada: Performance Management Network, 1997.

17. Edgar Schein. *The Corporate Culture Survival Guide.* San Francisco: Jossey-Bass, 1999, 117–18.

18. K. Nichols. The Crucial Edge of Reinvention: A Primer on Scoping and Measuring for Organizational Change. *Public Administration Quarterly*, 21 (4), 1997, 405–18.

19. Oliver Krause. Beyond BSC: A Process Based Approach to Performance Management. *Measuring Business Excellence*, 7 (3), 2003, 4–14.

20. Peter Senge. The Leader's New Work: Building Learning Organizations. *Sloan Management Review*, 31 (1), 1990, 3.

Appendix A

Sample Library Strategic Plans

The following library strategic plans are just a small sample of the plans produced in the last few years. These are not recommended as models of what to do but rather to illustrate the wide range of possibilities when preparing a strategic plan. One universal criticism of most of these plans is that very few strategies are articulated in the plan, but rather objectives are usually used as a "strategy." Remember that a strategy is designed to answer the question, "How are we going to accomplish the task of reaching the library's vision?," not "What are our objectives?"

Public Libraries

Evanston Public Library
http://www.evanston.lib.il.us/library/strategic-plan-00.html

Burlington Public Library
http://www.bpl.on.ca/whatsnew/building/buildingStrat.htm

Columbus Metropolitan Library
http://www.cml.lib.oh.us/new/strategicplan.cfm

The Guelph Public Library
http://www.library.guelph.on.ca/whatsnew.cfm?id=127

The Kitchener Public Library
http://www.kpl.org/ayl_strat_plan.shtml

Mission Viejo Library
http://cmvl.org/strategicplan.html

Morton Grove Public Library
http://www.webrary.org/inside/stratplan1.html

Mountain View Public Library
http://www.ci.mtnview.ca.us/citydepts/lib/li/strategic.htm

Pawtucket Public Library
http://www.pawtucketlibrary.org/strategicplan.htm

Sonoma County Library
http://www.sonoma.lib.ca.us/stratplan0.html

Academic Libraries

Appalachian State University
http://www.library.appstate.edu/geninfo/strategic_plan_2000-2005.html

Bond University, Australia
http://www.bond.edu.au/Library/documents/Library%20Strategic%20Plan%202004.pdf

California State University Northridge
http://library.csun.edu/susan.curzon/stratpln.html

Central Connecticut State University
http://www.ccsu.edu/AcadAffairs/strategicplan/Library.htm

Northeastern Illinois University
http://www.neiu.edu/~libstaff/planning/stratplan.html

Tufts University
http://www.library.tufts.edu/tisch/about/strategic_plan.htm

Syracuse University
http://libwww.syr.edu/information/strategicplan/

University of British Columbia
http://www.library.ubc.ca/home/planning/

University of Nebraska at Omaha
http://library.unomaha.edu/information/stratplan/index.php

Wake Forest University Baptist Medical Center
http://www.wfubmc.edu/library/strategic_plan/

Appendix B

Critique of a Library Strategic Plan

The challenge in formulating a set of strategies for a specific library is that librarians have little or no experience in taking a step back and considering that there are alternative ways (strategies) for delivering library services. Thus, it is not surprising that few library strategic plans actually identify the strategies that they will use to realize the library's vision. In the following sample strategic library plan, the statements that are made by the library are not in fact strategies (ways to accomplish an objective) but rather are simply a set of objectives that have been called strategies.

Our Vision

We are committed to meeting the information needs of our academic community; to providing effective, caring, and responsive service; to partnering with faculty in the education of our students; to developing the information competence skills of our students; and to fostering a love of reading and learning.

Our Strategic Directions

- The foremost provider of information resources to support the academic success of our students.

- The foremost provider of information resources to support the teaching and research of our faculty.

- A teaching library engaged in the development of the information research skills of our students.

- A preserver and developer of collections and of archives essential to faculty and student research.

- A center for independent, resource-based learning that promotes engagement with resources, studying, the seeking of knowledge; and the freedom of information.

Our Distinguishing Characteristics

The distinguishing characteristics of our library include a collection superbly tailored to our student and faculty needs, exemplary service to all our users, skillful and engaging instruction on information research skills, strong and continuous support from our users and friends, and a national reputation for excellence in librarianship and library service.

We Value:

- An outstanding, highly accessible, comprehensive university level collection.
- The freedom of information.
- The importance of reading.
- Effective teaching.
- Scholarly research.
- Being a vital part of the instructional program.
- Courteous, capable, and responsive service.
- Service to the greater community.
- Respect for our users and our colleagues.
- Ease of access to information and services.
- The effective application of technology and the effective use of resources.
- A comfortable, quiet, calm, safe, and clean library environment.
- The privacy of our users.
- Positive, open communication.
- Professionalism and pride in our work.
- Openness to new ideas and a willingness to change.
- A commitment to our own growth and development.
- Our professional ethics.

- Respect for diversity.
- Libraries that can change lives.

The Learning Outcomes for Our Students

We are committed to instilling in our students a lifelong commitment to learning, to the freedom of information, and to the search for knowledge. Specifically, we are committed to the following learning outcomes for our students:

- Highly skilled in information research.
- Confident and competent in the use of physical libraries.
- Confident and competent in the use of electronic libraries.

Index

Ackoff, Russell, 104
Adams, Scott, 13
Alakos, Amos, 103
Association of Research Libraries
   (ARL)
   LibQUAL+, 100

Balance, in performance measures
   absolute/relative, 115
   direct/indirect, 116
   leading/lagging, 116
   objective/subjective, 116
   performance/diagnostic, 115
   process/function oriented, 115
   social/economic, 116
Balanced scorecard, as management
   tool, 123, 126–30
   customer perspective, 126,
     127(fig.)
   financial perspective, 126,
     127(fig.)
   innovation and learning
     perspective, 126, 127(fig.)
   internal perspective, 126,
     127(fig.)
   library scorecard, 129, 130(fig.)
   Three Rs, 133(fig.)
Barrett, Richard, 20
Benchmarking, as management tool,
   109
Berra, Yogi, 22
Bhide, Amar, 26
Birinyi, Lazlo, 95
Block, Peter, 21
Bossidy, Lawrence A., 83

Brandenburger, Adam M., 25
Brigham Young University, sample
   mission statement, 16
Budgeting, as management tool,
   109–10
Budgets, 109
   line-item, 110
   performance, 110
   priority-based, 110
   program, 110
   zero-based, 110
Burke, James, 67
Butler, Meredith, 67

Campbell, Michael, 111
Carter, John C., 86
Choices, 59
Cognitive School
   Myers-Briggs instrument and, 36
   premises of, 36
Collins, David J., 47
Collins, Jim, 20
Competition, forces influencing,
   33–34, 34(fig.)
Competitive Advantage, 33
Competitive Strategy, 33
Configuration School, 29, 40
   premises of, 40
Consistency, provided by strategy, 7
   Coopers & Lybrand, PBP, 78
Core competencies, 26
CRITERIA, 77
Critical success factors, 78–79
Cromwell, Oliver, 132

145

Cultural School
   focus of, 38–39
Culture of assessment, 95–105
   initiatives for developing, 100–5
   obstacles to, 98–99
   performance measures in, 95–97
Customer intimacy, 45–46, 51(fig.)
Customer orientation, 48
Customer satisfaction measurement,
   as management tool, 109
Customer's voice, in culture of
   assessment, 100–1
Cuyahoga County Public Library,
   sample mission statement, 18

da Vinci, Leonardo, 61
Davis, Hiram, 67
De Gennaro, Richard, 61
Deane, Gary, 21
Decision analysis, 74–76
   decision tree, 74, 75(fig.)
   influence diagram, 74, 75(fig.)
Decision tree, 74, 75(fig.)
Dell, Michael, 4
Delphi studies, 71
"Delusional optimism," and decision
   making, 80
Design School
   criteria used in evaluation, 30
   premises of, 30–31
   SWOT analysis in, 30, 31
Differentiation, 34
   change service offerings, 49
   customer orientation, 48
   distribution, 49
   innovation, 48
   installed customer base, 49
   name, 49
   quality, 47–48
   support, 49
   technical superiority, 48
Direction, set by strategy, 7, 12–13
Distribution, 49

Drucker, Peter, 15, 35, 46, 65, 96
Duke University, sample mission
   statement, 17

Effort, focused by strategy, 7
Emerson, Ralph Waldo, 7
Entrepreneurial School
   premises of, 35
Environmental School
   premises, 39

Fifth Discipline, The, 37
Finlay, Joel, 23
Fitzgerald, F. Scott, 7
5 Whys, 15
5Ps, 69
Focus, 58
   geographic, 47
   market segments, 47
   product/service, 47
Force field analysis/diagram, 89–91,
   90(fig.)

Gaebler, Ted, 14, 115
Game theory, 73–74
   "Prisoner's Dilemma," 74
Games in organizations, 37–38
Gast, Walter, 15
Gast's Laws, 15
Goals and objectives, setting, 77–78
Gorman, Michael, 21
Grossmont Healthcare, sample
   mission statement, 18

Handy, Charles, 95
Heller, Robert, 6
Hout, Thomas M., 86
Hybrid library, 71

Implementation of strategy, 83–91
Influence diagram, 74, 75(fig.)
Innovation, 48
Innovative services, 45, 51(fig.)

Installed customer base, 49
Ittner, Chris, 78

Kaplan, Robert S., 123, 129
Kitchener Public Library, sample
    mission statement, 18
Kotter, John, 109
Kress, Donald, 97
Kuhn, Thomas, xi

Lakos, Amos, 98, 99
Larcher, David, 78
Learning organization, defined, 103
Learning School
    premises of, 36–37
Lewin, Kurt, 89
Liberating the Corporate Soul, 20
Library strategic plan
    critique of, 141–43
    samples
        academic libraries, 140
        public libraries, 139–40
LibQUAL+, 100
Libraries, perceived roles of, 22–23
Line-item budgeting, 110
Lowry, Charles, xi

Management measurement cycle
    (fig.), 66, 83, 96
Management tools
    balanced scorecard, 123, 126–29
        library scorecard, 129–30
    benchmarking, 109
    budgeting, 109–10
    customer satisfaction
        measurement, 109
    mission and vision statements,
        109
    performance measurement,
        111–23
    performance prism, 130–32
    strategic planning, 109, 111
    Three Rs of Performance, 132–34

McLean, Neil, 111, 113
Mcdina County District Library,
    sample mission statement, 18
Mintzberg, Henry, 30
Mission, 13–19. See also Mission
    and vision statements
    benefits of clarifying, 16
Mission and vision statements, 14,
    21–22
    failings in, 15
    as management tool, 109
    samples, 16–19
Mobil NA Marketing and Refining,
    45
Monitoring/updating strategies
    culture of assessment, 95–107
    management tools, 109–37
Montgomery, Cynthia A., 47
Mooers's Law, 48
Moore, Thomas, 57
Multnomah County Library, sample
    mission statement, 18
Myers-Briggs instrument, 36

Nalebuff, Barry J., 25
Naperville Public Libraries, sample
    mission statement, 18
National Institute of Standards and
    Technology (NIST) , sample
    mission statement, 18
Needs and expectations, 58
Neely, Andy, 130
Norton, David, 123

Operational excellence, 44, 51(fig.)
Organization, defined by strategy,
    6–7
Organization's voice, in culture of
    assessment, 103–5
Osborne, David, 14, 115

PDCA. See Plan, Do, Check, and
    Act cycle (PDCA)

Performance Effectiveness
Management System (PEMS),
104
Performance measures/measurement
approach to, 114(fig.)
in culture of assessment, 95–97
definition template, 117(fig.)
framework, 113(fig.)
hierarchy of, 112(fig.)
library, 118–23, 118(fig.),
120–22(fig.)
as management tool, 111–23
obstacles to use of, 98–99
potential, 124–25
system attributes
alignment, 115
balance, 115
clarity of purpose, 115
focus, 58, 115
regular refinement, 116
vigorous indicators, 116
Performance prism, 130–32,
131(fig.)
capabilities, 131
processes, 131
stakeholder contribution, 131
stakeholder satisfaction, 131
strategies, 131
Personalization
customized, 48
standardized, 48
tailored, 48
Perspectives. *See under* Balanced
scorecard, as management tool
Peters, Paul Evans, 72
Peters, Tom, 91, 104
Phipps, Shelley, 103
Plan, 11, 25, 79–80
defined, 4
facets of, 12–13
Plan, Do, Check, and Act cycle
(PDCA), 65–66, 65(fig.),
66(fig.)

Planning process. *See* Strategic
planning process
Planning Programming Budgeting
System (PPBS), 110
Planning School
steps in process, 31–32
SWOT analysis in 31
Politics in an organization, 38
Porter, Michael, 5, 25, 29, 33
Positioning School, 33–34
premises of, 33
Power School
games in organizations, 37–38
premises of, 38
Priority and performance evaluation
(PAPE), 100
Priority Based Planning (PBP), 78
Priority-based budgeting (PBB), 110
Process, 59–60
voice of, in culture of assessment,
102–3
Processes
analytical, 33
collective, 38
conception, 30
emergent, 36
formal, 31
mental, 36
negotiation, 37
reactive, 39
transformation, 40
visionary, 35
Program budgeting, 110

Quality, 47–48

Reinventing Government, 14]
Renaud, Robert, 100
Richland County Free Library (SC) ,
sample mission statement, 18
Riggs, Donald, xi

San Diego Public Library, sample mission statement, 18
Santa Clara County Library, sample mission statement, 18
Scenario planning, 71–73
    Delphi studies, 71
    gaming and simulation, 72–73
    trend extrapolation, 72
Schein, Edgar, 134
Scope, 89
Schwartz, Peter, 71
Senge, Peter, 21, 37, 103, 135
SEPTEMBER, 70
Sertillanges, A. G., 11
Service/product usage, 50
Shell Oil, 72
Shinseki, Eric, General, 3
Shuman, Bruce, 72
St. Joseph County Public Library Mission Statement, sample, 17
Staff's voice, in culture of assessment, 101–2
Stevenson, Howard H., xi
Stoffle, Carla J., 100
Strategic options/choices, 52
    differentiation, 47–49
    focus, 47, 58
    service/product usage, 59
    synergy, 50–52
Strategic planning
    alternatives, 67–76
    continuous, 57
    defined, 57–60
    implementation of, 83–91
    long-range versus, 62
    as management tool, 109, 111
    measurement of success, 58
    members involved, 58
    positive outcomes of, 62–64
    process, 58
    process options, 46–52, 65–80
    "seven deadly sins," 32
    systematic, 57
    value of, 61–64

Strategic Planning for Library Managers, xi
Strategic planning process
    core concepts of, 13–26
    methods of, 89–91
    options, 65–80
    participants in, 86–87
    purposes of, 11–12
    requirements for, 88
    starting, 86
    tips, 87
Strategic thought, schools of
    Cognitive School, 29, 36
    Configuration School, 29, 40
    Cultural School, 29, 38–39
    Design School, 29, 30–31
    Entrepreneurial School, 29, 35
    Environmental School, 29, 39
    Learning School, 29, 36–37
    Planning School, 29, 31–32
    Positioning School, 29, 33–34
    Power School, 29, 37–38
Strategic value disciplines, 51(fig.)
Strategies, 24–26. See also Strategy formulation; Strategy implementation
    cost leadership, 34
    defined, 3–8
    differentiation, 34, 47–49
    focus, 34, 47, 58
    limits of, 6–8
    monitoring/updating, 93–137
    need for, 11–27
    pattern, 5, 25
    perspective, 5, 25
    plan, 4, 25
    ploy, 5
    position, 5, 25
    school of thought about, 29–41
    types of, 43–52
    U.S. Army, 6
Strategy formulation, 76–77
    CRITERIA, 77
Strategy implementation, 83

barriers to, 84–85
reasons for failure of, 85
Strengths, Weaknesses,
    Opportunities, and Threats
    (SWOT), 30, 31, 67–69,
    67(fig.), 68(fig.), 70–71
Sullivan, Gordon R., 3
Sun Tzu, *The Art of War*, 3
SWOT. *See* Strengths, Weaknesses,
    Opportunities, and Threats
    (SWOT)
Synergy, 50
System dynamic models (mental
    models), 76

TEMPLES, 69–70
Tennant, Roy, 43
Three Rs of Performance, 132–34,
    133(fig.)
    reach, 132
    resources, 132
    results, 133
Tichy, Noel, 88

UCLA, sample mission statement,
    17
University of Arizona library,
    PEMS, 104

University of British Columbia
    Library, sample strategic plan,
    80

Values, 19–21
    purpose of, 21
    questions about core, 20
    "value audit instrument," 20
Veldof, Jerilyn R., 100
Vision, 21–24. *See also* Mission and
    vision statements
    barriers to changing, 24
    developing , 22–24
Voice of customer. *See* Customer's
    voice, in culture of assessment
Voice of library staff members. *See*
    Staff's voice, in culture of
    assessment
Voice of organization. *See*
    Organization's voice, in
    culture of assessment
Voice of process. *See* Process, voice
    of, in culture of assessment
von Neumann, John, 73

Waterman, Bob, 91, 104
Wilde, Clare, 111, 113

Zero-based budgeting, 110

About the Author

JOSEPH R. MATTHEWS is an internationally renowned expert on information technology and strategic planning and president of JRM Consulting in Carlsbad, California. Titles currently in print include *Library Information Systems* (with Thomas R. Kochtanek, 2002), *The Bottom Line* (2002), *Measuring for Results* (2003), and *Technology Planning* (2004), all with Libraries Unlimited.